RICHMOND PARK

The Walker's Guide

IN THE SAME SERIES

Hampstead Heath: *The Walker's Guide*

The Thames from Hampton to Richmond Bridge: *The Walker's Guide*

The Thames from Richmond to Putney Bridge: *The Walker's Guide*

Windsor Great Park: *The Walker's Guide* (in preparation)

RICHMOND PARK

The Walker's Guide

David McDowall

with sketch maps & line drawings by

Angela Kidner

COVER: *Richmond Park*, Charles Sharland, 1911.

First edition 1996; this revised and enlarged edition 2006
Published by David McDowall
31 Cambrian Road, Richmond, Surrey TW10 6JQ
www.davidmcdowall.com

British Library Cataloguing in Publication Data
A catalogue record for this book is available from the British Library

ISBN 0-9527847-4-2
ISBN 978-0-9527847-4-6

Designed and typeset in Monotype Octavian and Formata by Peter Moore
Printed in China

Contents

Maps

Illustrations

Line drawings

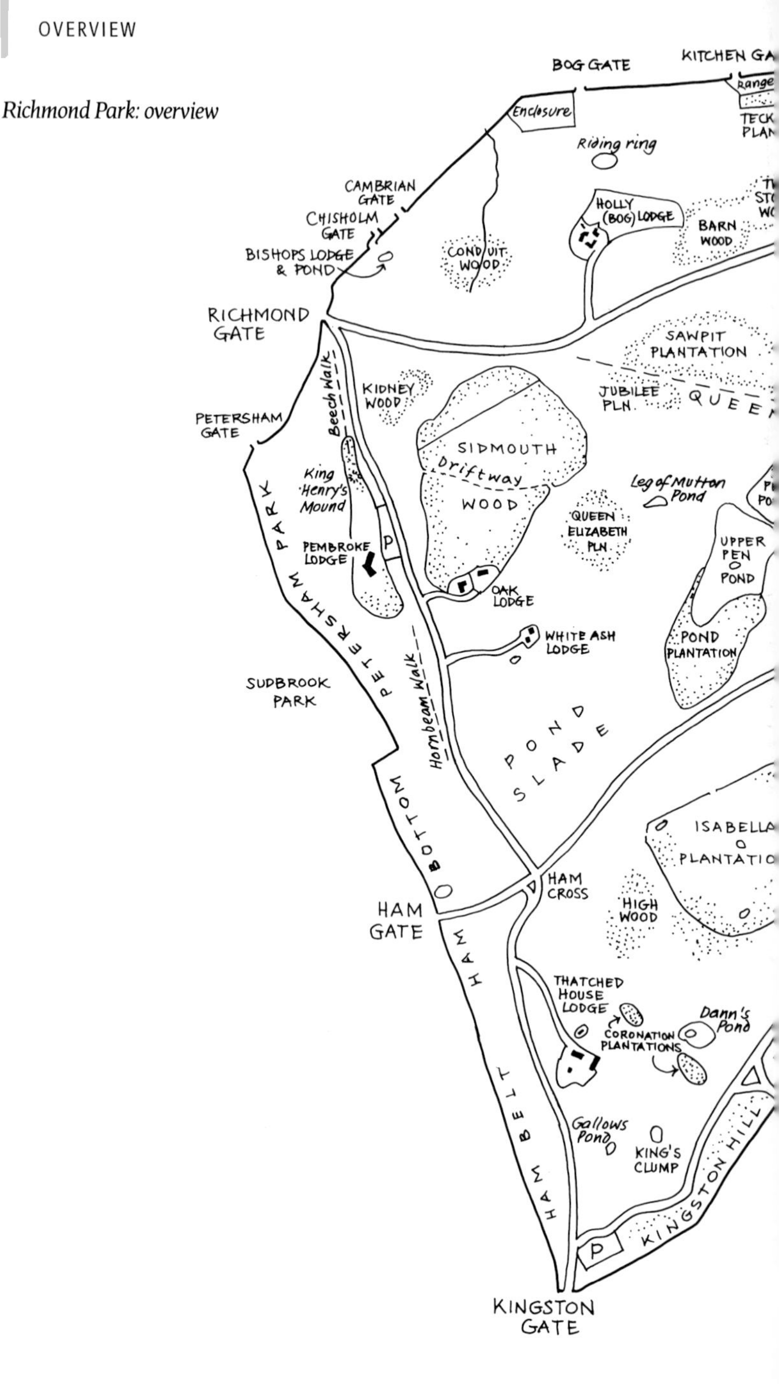

Richmond Park: overview

GATE

Adam's Pond

ROEHAMPTON PLN.

ROEHAMPTON GATE

SHEEN CROSS WOOD

P

GOLF COURSE

Old deer pen

VICTORY PLN.

THE WHITE LODGE

BEVERLEY BROOK

KINGS FARM PLANTATION

HYDE PARK NURSERY

TREEBOX WOOD

CHOHOLE GATE

SPANKERS HILL WOOD

GOLF COURSE

P

P

ENARY

Martin's Pond

ROBIN HOOD GATE

NCE ARLES NNEY

BROOMFIELD HILL WOOD

P

E

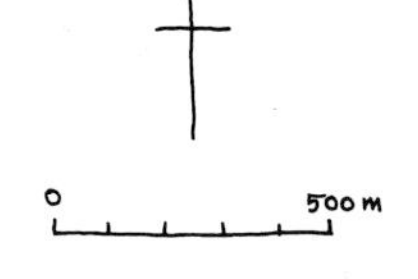

Acknowledgements

I am indebted to those who have already written on the park. Most of this is in published form but reports commissioned by the Royal Parks have also been consulted. I owe a particular debt to the survey carried out by Dr Tom Greeves, *Richmond Park, London: Archaeological Survey* (The Royal Parks, unpublished mimeograph, London 1992). I also owe a great debt to the generosity and unrivalled knowledge of John Cloake, Richmond's outstanding local historian. At the Local Studies Collection, Richmond Public Library, Jane Baxter has always been extraordinarily efficient and helpful, locating materials in the collection and kindly supplying most of the illustrations. At the National Archives I was able to look at the two earliest maps of Richmond Park, those of Nicholas Lane and Elias Allen, indicating field names at the time of enclosure. R.G.Phillip kindly allowed me to quote from F.D.Ommaney's *The House in the Park* and Routledge kindly allowed me to quote from *The Autobiography of Bertrand Russell* (George Allen and Unwin Ltd, 1967) vol.i, pp.13, 30. In the park itself I have had nothing but courtesy and helpfulness from its staff. They have shared their knowledge and tried to correct my misunderstandings. With this revised edition, I am particularly grateful to Simon Richards, the superintendent, and Nigel Reeve, community ecologist for the Royal Parks. Both read through the text meticulously, providing extra important information and drawing my attention to factual errors.

It was in preparing a similar book on Hampstead Heath that I began to learn to look at trees and other flora. My teacher was my co-author, Deborah Wolton, and if I have learnt anything, I almost certainly owe it to her.

Thanks, too, to my dear wife, Elizabeth, for reading the text, and checking for inadequate explanations, *non sequiturs* and typographical errors. A spouse can get away with a degree of critical candour intolerable from anyone else, and the end product is all the better for her truthfulness.

I owe a double debt to Angela and Patrick Kidner. They tested each walk for the first edition, regardless of the weather, giving me both encouragement and comments in perfect measure. Angela's sketch maps have given this book a very special quality and I am greatly indebted to her. Finally, Peter Moore has brought to this edition his usual skill. When a reviewer recently described these guides as 'exquisitely self-published', I knew that the plaudits rightly belong to Peter and Angela who have given my efforts such elegance.

THE ILLUSTRATIONS

I am very grateful to the London Transport Museum for permission to use Charles Sharland's *Richmond Park,* 1911, as the cover illustration; to Daniel Hearsum, who manages Pembroke Lodge, for the photograph from his archive of the GHQ (Phantom) Liaison Regiment on p.131; and to the London Borough of Richmond upon Thames Local Studies Collection for the provision of all the remaining illustrations, except that of Gallows Conduit, and the sketches provided by Angela Kidner and Deborah Wolton.

Introduction

Richmond Park is one of the largest enclosed parks in Britain, over 2,500 acres in size. It is also the least disturbed expanse of land in the Greater London area with prehistoric, medieval as well as more modern traces of human activity. This is because Charles I enclosed the land as a royal hunting park between 1632 and 1637. Very little ground disturbance has happened since then, except during the two world wars. Consequently visible traces of previous land use may be found in many parts of the park, a real rarity in south-eastern England. Furthermore, Charles' enclosure could not be done without compensating tenants with holdings inside what he intended to empark. A map was drawn by a Nicholas Lane. This map survives, providing unique information concerning the landscape as it existed in the 1630s.

This guide is devoted to exploring the landscape on foot, recognizing aspects of its ecology and finding traces of the past uses to which this land was once put. It is intended as a walking companion, both for those who already habitually use the park but also for newcomers who wish to enjoy the more concealed delights the park has to offer. These include both the more obvious aspects of the ecology and features which are often subtle but distinct enough that with imagination one can reconstruct in the mind's eye what things may once have looked like. Some features may seem unprepossessing, but if your experience is like mine, the more you walk the park the more pleasure they will give and your feeling for the park will, I hope, be enriched in the process.

I have been on a learning curve since the first edition of this book, subtitled *The Walker's Historical Guide*, published almost ten years ago. While I have retained and revised the walks which featured in that book, I now include a preliminary chapter on the common flora that can be seen as one walks and how they have traditionally been used. Where the information started to feel footnote-ish I consigned it to appendices, where all except the relentlessly dogged will, I trust, find some satisfaction. I have also devoted fresh space to trying to extract more information about the historic landscape from Nicholas Lane's enclosure map of 1637.

Walks are illustrated where necessary with sketch maps. Numbers in brackets in the text indicate that the features to which they refer may be located on the relevant sketch map. There is an overall reference sketch map of the whole park on pages 8-9, and a map in two sections on pp.64-66 intended to assist in relating Lane's enclosure map to the park as it is today.

Towards the end of the book I have written a short polemic about our custodianship of this great park. The more I explore Richmond Park the more I lament what has been lost and the dismal prospect of possible further diminishment in the future. It is my hope that your appreciation of this wonderful and unique landscape will be transformed through this book, as it was for me while researching it and that you may, just possibly, agree with me about the priorities we should adopt to help safeguard the park's future. My delight, now I know more than when I wrote the first edition in 1996, is constantly tinged with sadness at what we have unthinkingly thrown away.

Finally, this book does not belong on a shelf but in your coat pocket. Please give it hard use, however battered it may become. A pristine copy is a dead copy, of use to neither man nor beast.

David M^c^Dowall
Richmond, February 2006

Reading the landscape

Wherever one goes in Richmond Park, there is a real pleasure in understanding, however simply, the making of the park's ecology and humankind's interaction with it. So, before undertaking any walks, it may be worthwhile casting a quick eye over this introduction. Appendices provide more information regarding the trees, the deer, the birds and the ponds.

FORMATION OF THE LANDSCAPE

It is useful to know something of the geological sequence which determined the flora of the park. About 80 million years ago the land lay under a warm sea and a fine deposit of what became chalk was laid on the ocean bed. It is about 200 metres thick. Sixty million years ago, the sea laid down a fresh deposit of fine mud, London clay. About 30 million years ago, the precursor of the river Thames, but at least ten times its size, rose in the Cotswolds and flowed north-east across the Vale of Oxford. Over a long period between 20 and 5 million years ago, the valley through which the Thames eventually flowed was created, in a sequence of earth movements which created folds in the chalk, and also threw up the Alps and Himalayas.

Above all, it was the Ice Age which produced the Thames Valley. Two million years ago, ice cut the Goring Gap through the hills at Maidenhead, creating a new river route. At first the water flowed across the Vale of St Albans but with the Great Ice Age of 450,000 years ago, its route was forced southwards to avoid the icecap (which reached as far south as the North Circular Road). For a period of 200,000 years there were repeated phases of glaciation and thaw, which cut the Thames Valley, leaving terraces on each side of the river. All these terraces are made up of debris brought down by the river. Much of that debris is inhospitable for many plants and leads to a specific type of environment with its own characteristic vegetation.

It is the poor quality of the soil which explains why so much of it was still common land or 'waste' when Charles I cast a covetous eye across it in the early 1630s. Had it been nutrient-rich it would have been intensively farmed and thus unlikely that Charles would have sought to make it a deer park. Some of the soil was worth cultivating, though it was a good deal less fertile than the clay soils of the lower slopes of the valley, while most of the land was simply not worth the effort. But the 'waste' was not waste in the sense we now understand the word. It was still valuable, for what it could provide. It remains valuable today because it is an increasingly rare environment in Britain. Current policy is to maintain and regenerate where necessary the indigenous species of the park and to avoid planting exotics. It is, of course, the only policy that makes sense if we are to cherish and enrich what we have inherited. These acid grasslands are, or should be, a priority for us if we are remotely concerned with conservation.

FLORA OF THE LANDSCAPE

Trees are, of course, the most noticeable flora of the landscape. The most common 'pioneers', if they escape the attentions of grazing livestock, are birch, hawthorn, oak, elm (now reduced to suckers), ash and two exotics, sycamore and rhododendron. Birch, with its prolific windborne seed, is usually the first coloniser on vacant ground, particularly this kind of poor soil, while the other tree species tend to succeed it, as the woodland it has pioneered becomes mature. Oak usually becomes the dominant species, while the birch cannot regenerate under another species' canopy and therefore colonises afresh on some open turf-free area. Hawthorn will also colonise in the open and is notorious for turning open grassland into scrub. Some hawthorns in the park are 200 years old or even older, a very substantial age for the species. Hawthorn and oak have both been here in symbiotic relationship for many centuries. In some of the woodland the presence of veteran hawthorns beneath an oak canopy suggests that the oak woodland grew through thorn scrub. Whether in scrub or in a hedgerow, the oak seedling often escaped livestock grazing by growing through hawthorn, hence an old saw: 'the hawthorn is the mother of the oak'. Other trees in the park include alder and willow, that like to have their roots in very wet soil, and ash, which will often outdo oak on wet slopes.

Here, in the park, the mature woodland is predominantly oak, of which roughly 800 trees are 'veterans', more than 350 years old. Of these approximately half are pollards, trees once routinely cropped above the browse line. No one visiting the park can fail to be struck by the beauty of these veterans:

> '... those grey, gnarled, low-browed, knock-kneed, bowed, bent, misshapen oak men that stand waiting and watching century after century.... They look as if they had been at the beginning and making of the world, and they will probably see its end.'
>
> Francis Kilvert, 22 April 1876

Kilvert was an irredeemable romantic, and it is undoubtedly romanticism that these venerable trees inspire. The oak is the pre-eminent tree of European mythology. In Lower Austria a church stands on a once pagan site, dedicated to 'Mary of the Three Oaks'. The name harks back to a pre-Christian era. When it comes to trees, the pagans had discrimination.

Before Charles' enclosure, very few oak trees would have been allowed to grow old, because they would all have been farmed. They were grown for cropping. It is claimed that Henry VIII was the first English king to delight in veteran trees, symbols of continuity and stability in the landscape and, by association, similar attributes in the dynastic owners of the landscape. It is from Henry's time that one can date the peculiarly English affection for landscapes with ancient trees. Since his day there has often been a conscious desire to preserve ancient trees, and this became much more pronounced with the development of landscaped parks in the eighteenth century. For their antiquity England's timber resources must be unrivalled. When the roof of Westminster Hall was damaged by enemy action in 1941, it was to the same estate in Sussex, which had provided the original oak in the late fourteenth century, that the restorers had recourse.

Romanticism apart, it is helpful to know a few rudimentary facts about trees in the park. The veteran trees in particular constitute an extraordinarily valuable ecological asset. In the words of Oliver Rackham, the countryside historian:

> 'An old tree, especially a pollard, is a world of different habitats each with its special plants and animals: bats roosting in the hollow trunk; hole-nesting birds in smaller cavities; many special beetles and spiders [*one might also add fungi*] in the red-rotted heartwood of the trunk; peculiar lichens on the ridges and beneath overhangs of old bark. Any old tree should be treasured, for ten thousand young trees do not provide these habitats.'

The rotting heartwood often found in these old trees provides a habitat for two extremely rare click beetles, the rusty (*Elater ferrugineus*) and the cardinal (*Ampedus cardinalis*). The park is an exceptionally important site for such invertebrates.

As they pass their prime, oak trees die back. Many of the oldest oaks can become top heavy or unbalanced as each dies back unevenly. Restoring such ancient pollards and maidens requires skill and judgement. Amputate too much and the tree will suffer trauma and die. Do nothing and a strong wind may fell it. Their preservation is a priority.

Were it not for livestock – today deer, but previously cattle, horses and sheep – the landscape would be almost entirely wooded, principally with oak and hawthorn, clearings occurring only where trees had died and there was a temporary absence of successors. But for at least 2,000 years before the enclosure large areas of this landscape had probably been heathland or acid grassland, the result of being grazed by livestock. So this landscape is not only historic, but prehistoric too.

One can still find classic heath and acid grassland plants. Gorse, or furze, must have been much more widespread in the drier areas before the advent of the deer, which seem to mind its prickles less than other grazers. Bracken is also indigenous to the nutrient-poor landscape here. Invasive though it is, it should command our respect for its successful longevity. It is significantly older than almost any other plant cover, except for moss and lichen, having made its first appearance about 360 million years ago, about 100 million years before the arrival of dinosaurs. Some humility, therefore, is in order, for by comparison we are complete parvenus. As you walk you may notice areas of bracken that have been cut and heaped into composting piles, for use in the Isabella plantation. Elsewhere, some areas of bracken are rolled, insufficient to kill it, but sufficient to thin it and allow other grassland species to grow through, creating greater variety and thus a more diverse wildlife habitat.

The landscape grasses are divided between the finer bladed ones in the nutrient-poor acid soils of the upland area of the park and the coarser grasses that prefer the nutrient-enriched areas, notably the slopes down to Petersham (the more obvious of these are listed at Appendix 1), and around car parks and other areas of dog fouling. Some areas of the park are characterised by anthills, host to sub-communities of mosses, lichens, fungi and small flowering plants. Richmond Park constitutes easily the most important acid grassland in the Greater London area.

TRADITIONAL USES OF THE FLORA IN RICHMOND PARK

Today we walk across the landscape for its beauty, with scarcely a thought for the usefulness of what grows here. Until the park enclosure (and for a considerable time after it) no one living locally could possibly ignore the value of what this 'waste' produced, essential items for food and shelter. Here are a few reminders of just how valuable this produce was and of how landscape management affected the way the land then looked.

At the time of the 1637 enclosure (see map pp.64-66) there were a number of enclosed woods and also open common areas with some tree cover. Woodland management was a sophisticated skill, well established by the thirteenth century, with exploitation and conservation held in symbiotic balance. That is why we still have so many ancient oak trees, both 'maidens' (standard trees, their principal shoot never lopped) and pollards, once routinely cropped above the browse line, but largely let go since 1637.

Trees were the most important asset of the waste. They yielded two different commodities: timber and underwood, a distinction to which we are unaccustomed today. For medieval man the difference was clear. Timber meant tree trunks and very seldom anything else. These 'maidens', it was hoped, would grow tall and straight. Yet they would rarely be allowed to grow to anything like the size we see now. Most oak trees would be felled after about 35 years, when the trunks were about 25cm in diameter, easily sufficient as load-bearing beams in most buildings. They would be worked 'green', the bark being 'flawed' (a local Surrey word) from the trunk after felling and sold to a tannery, probably the one in Kingston. Oak had to be worked green, because once it started to dry it hardened so much that it was a nightmare to work with. The trunk would be 'scappled', or squared, with axe and adze to produce a 'boxed heart' before use. Those timbers required for braces, rafters or as joists would be halved or quartered, either sawn or cleft and squared with an adze. Cleaving might produce waviness in the final product but had the advantage of respecting the grain and therefore the strength and durability of the end product.

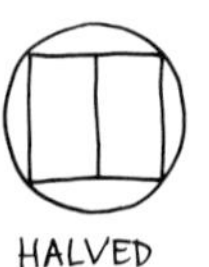

In the Middle Ages there was reluctance to grow oak any larger than 35cm diameter because of the difficulty of moving fallen tree trunks and then of cutting them lengthwise. Sawing became more common in the Tudor period, presumably because of improved technology.

It is difficult to overestimate the value of oak wood, on account of its strength and also its resilience against the elements. Oak was sufficiently important for ships that a phrase was coined in the eighteenth century concerning the oak: *Britanniae Decus et Tutamen*, in English, 'The Glory and Protection of Britain', later filched by the Royal Mint to put on one pound coins. A report to Parliament in 1763 on the shortage of oak for the navy was entitled *Hearts of Oak: The British Bulwark*. One gets the message.

Yet do not believe that Britain ran out of good oak because of the demands of the navy. Although much oak was used for house building and forges in the sixteenth and seventeenth centuries, the shortage that the Admiralty repeatedly complained about chiefly concerned its own reluctance to procure oak on the open market, rather than scrounging it free or at knock-down prices from

Crown land. Even in the late eighteenth century, there was three or four times as much merchant as war shipping. Furthermore, the tonnage of timber ships built between 1800 and 1860 equals all previous British shipbuilding put together. Had there been a genuine shortage, this output could not have happened. The truth is that most commercially grown oak was for housing and other domestic purposes. Indeed, until the late eighteenth century oak accounted for 95 per cent of domestic timber.

In the nineteenth century new plantations, usually with only one or two species, were established in Richmond Park. Unlike plantations established for economic purposes elsewhere, for example on previous heathland, these were often created in areas where trees were already growing and were nurtured as a permanent ornament to the landscape.

'Underwood' grew either as scrub hardwood, fit only for fuel, or in a managed form either as coppice or as wood cropped off either pollards or standards. With the latter, the carpenter would chose an angled branch for a specific task to which it was suited. The angle would always prove infinitely stronger than any carpenter's joint, however carefully this was made. Medieval carpenters understood their material very well indeed.

Use of underwood by the manor's tenants would be strictly controlled and rationed by the manor steward. Underwood fell into defined categories depending on the purpose in hand, for example, *firebote, hedgebote, housebote, cartbote, stilebote, gatebote* 'and other customary botes'. *Bote*, Norman-French for a bundle, was the term used for the rationed entitlement of tenants to timber and underwood.

Coppice, periodically cut at ground level, had to be fenced in, to protect it from grazing livestock. Strongly favoured trees for coppice were ash, hazel, sallow, field maple and hornbeam. Most would be harvested simply as fuel faggots, or for turning into charcoal. By 1300 London's inhabitants consumed 140,000 tons of wood annually, for warmth and for cooking. Some of that wood almost certainly came from coppice here, probably taken down to Mortlake to be conveyed by barge to the city. Woodland on any manorial estate was vital, but especially so in the vicinity of London, even if coalmining progressively relieved the stress on wood fuel production from the sixteenth century onwards. Ash, strong and springy, would provide most of the wood for farm implements, stakes and so forth. Hazel yielded shoots that not only split true down the middle but could also be woven to and fro without breaking, thus being the ideal material for hurdles for livestock pens, wattle for housing or for plashing hedgerows. Sallow (goat and grey willow) was desirable because it grew whippy lengths rapidly, up to four metres in a season. They, too, would be used for 'rattle-and-dab', as wattle-and-daub was locally known. Hornbeam was used very little except for fuel faggots, for it gives off great heat. Often known as 'hardbeam', it was avoided for other purposes since its hardness blunted a carpenter's tools very quickly. Virtually the only use to which it could be put was for axles or gears, on account of its extreme durability.

Coppice would usually be divided into sections and cropped at ground level in rotation every seven to fifteen years. The 'stools' quickly regenerated and lost none of their vigour. Occasionally coppice grew alongside timber trees, but one had to be careful not to shade coppice and thus slow down its productivity. One can see an example in Deane's Coppice, now part of Two Storm Wood. The coppice stools have now gone but you can still see a few old oak maidens, which must have stood above the coppice 400 years ago.

Before the invention of barbed-wire in the second half of the nineteenth century, hawthorn was highly valued for its enclosure properties, its thorns acting as a deterrent. So it was the ideal hedgerow plant and, indeed, its name means 'enclosure thorn' in Anglo-Saxon. Other hardwoods grew in the hedgerows, notably oak, ash and elm, benefiting from the protection offered by thorn hedge. Once noticed, a tree would be protected from grazing until it grew above the browse line. These trees were then 'polled' or 'pollarded', for their wood above the browse line on a regular basis, like coppice. The first poll would take place when a tree was about thirty years old and then usually once every seven to ten years.

Pollards usually indicate two kinds of landscape features: either old hedgerow lines, which abound in the park, or 'wood pasture', an open landscape where livestock were allowed to graze between mature trees. One can see traces of this landscape in High Wood, once known as Black Heath, on the west side of the Isabella Plantation. This wood pasture is very old indeed and has very possibly never been put under the plough. A famous hedgerow pollard was the 'Shrew Ash' (see p.168) grown on the southern hedgerow of Ashen Close, which finally collapsed in 1987. Field maple was popular as a hedgerow plant, for its wood is very fine grained, ideal for turning on a lathe and popular for drinking bowls, or 'mazers'. An ancient field maple may be found in the narrow neck between the Isabella Plantation and Prince Charles' Spinney (Tree No.1384, if you think you have found it).

Furze or gorse was once highly valued, but its extent is now greatly diminished by grazing deer. It was used in hedgerows and for fuel, particularly for bread ovens on account of the high temperatures that could quickly be achieved. In lean years furze would be pounded and fed to livestock. It was sufficiently valued that strict rules would apply to commoners regarding seasonal cutting, to ensure fair distribution and adequate regeneration. It was also used for drying clothing. Its prickles acted as a grip and when in flower (practically the whole year around) its coconut-vanilla scent was imparted to freshly washed linen. Finally, it provided concealment behind which young lovers could find intimacy:

> 'Yonder came the smell of the gorse, so nutty,
> Gold-like and warm: it's the prime of May.
> Better than mortar, brick and putty,
> It's God's house on a blowing day.'
>
> George Meredith, *Juggling Jerry*

Like many plants, furze inspired superstition. Visiting an old woman in Anglesey in 1840, the wife of a local MP found her in bed, enclosed by furze which, the old woman claimed, 'kept the fairies from plaguing her, spilling her tea and souring her milk'. Do not mock. You never know.

Rushes were used for making baskets, plaiting into ropes and cordage, mats, and also for rush-bottomed chairs, the classic cottage furniture of Surrey. They were probably used as roofing material also. Those who have ever attended a Harvest Thanksgiving service and sung the full seven verses of 'All Things Bright and Beautiful' (written in 1848) must have wondered about the apparently idiotic assertion: 'The rushes by the water we gather every day'. Well, it was not just for fun. The pith of the soft rush, common in the park, was widely used for making rush-lights, the source of illumination in many cottages well into the nineteenth century. As Gilbert White in Selborne wrote in the mid-eighteenth century:

> 'The rushes are in best condition in the height of summer.... Decayed labourers, women and children, make it their business to procure and prepare them. As soon as they are cut they must be flung into water, and kept there; for otherwise they will dry and shrink, and the peel will not run. At first a person would find it no easy matter to divest a rush of its peel or rind, so as to leave one regular, even rib from top to bottom that may support the pith.... When these *junci* are

> thus prepared, they must lie out on the grass to be bleached, and take the dew for some nights and afterwards dried in the sun. Some address is required in dipping these rushes in the scalding fat or grease.... A good rush, which measured in length two feet four inches and a half, being minuted, burnt for only three minutes short of an hour: and a rush still of greater length has been known to burn one hour and a quarter. These rushes give good clear light.'

The poor may also have gathered purple moor grass from the wetter areas and made stiff brushes from its long stems. These stems could also be twisted together to make durable cordage.

Bracken was used as litter for both humans and livestock until the sixteenth century, when even the poorest people began to sleep in beds off the ground. It was also used for tinder and as kindling for fires and, when burnt to ash, mixed with animal fat and used as a crude soap. Many believed that pulling up or burning bracken influenced the weather. In August 1636, exactly the time that the park was being enclosed, Charles I was planning to travel thorough Staffordshire. On his instruction his lord chamberlain wrote to the county sheriff:

> 'Sir, His Majesty taking notice of an opinion entertained in Staffordshire that the burning of Ferne doth draw down rain and being desirous that the country and himself may enjoy fair weather as long as he remains in those parts, His Majesty hath commanded me to write unto you, to cause all burning of Ferne to be forborne, until His Majesty be passed the county.'

It is easy to forget that until roads were surfaced, rainfall could render any journey a nightmare. If Charles himself did not actually admit to believing this superstition, he was certainly not taking any chances.

Heather must have grown here also, for example on 'Little Heath Common' by the Bog Gate and on the Black Heath by

Ladderstile Gate. Like furze and bracken, it would have been used for fuel, fodder and bedding. Heather is extremely vulnerable to trampling and was probably eradicated by grazing deer, except for one tiny patch, midway between the Isabella and Pond Plantations.

Like the furze, the heather would also have been a food resource for bees. Bee-keeping was a means to supplement peasant family income. The hive, or skep, might be made of willow withies from the osier beds down by the river. Or a more rough-and-ready hive could be made out of the rushes and grasses growing here. The honey was a valued sweetener, while the wax would be made into candles.

The grasslands would have been used primarily for grazing. Commoners would have been rationed in the number of livestock they could put out onto the common, known as the stint, hence our phrase 'don't stint yourself'. Commoners were usually allowed to exceed their stint, on payment of a fine. But these lands would have also been used for 'turbary', the customary but again controlled right of cutting turfs, principally for the roofing of the poorer tenants' hovels.

In the autumn the swine of the manor would be put into the oakwoods to feed off the mast, a sufficiently important food resource that it had its own term, 'pannage', meticulously assessed in the Domesday Book.

Finally, even the ground could be of use. The river gravel and sand of the upland landscape were useful for building and for carriageways. We do not know when gravel was first extracted but we do know that the Pen Ponds, both probably dug before the end of the seventeenth century, were dug not only as part of the drainage system but also for their gravel, and gravel pits explain many of the smaller dips in the landscape.

The prehistoric and ancient sites

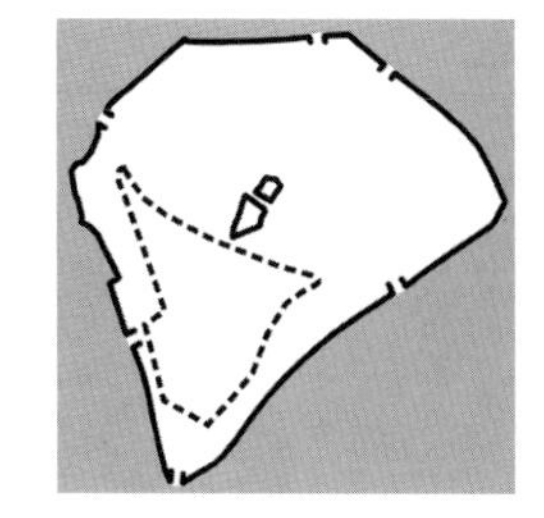

Distance 7km: 2.5 hours

ONLY UNDERTAKE THIS WALK BETWEEN MID-DECEMBER AND MAY WHEN GROUND COVER IS MINIMAL.

Start: Pembroke Lodge car park.
Please note that dogs are not admitted into Pembroke Lodge grounds.
Proceed northwards (i.e in the direction of Richmond Gate) from the car park, following the perimeter fence of Pembroke Lodge, ignore the first pedestrian entrance (50m) and enter the Pembroke Lodge estate by its northern gate (350m approx from the car park). Pass through the 'Laburnum Walk' and you find yourself facing King Henry VIII's Mound (1), see map on p.30.

This is the highest point in the park. Writing in 1835, Edward Jesse, Deputy Surveyor of the Royal Parks (see Walk No.7), was probably the first to recognize the likely existence of prehistoric barrows. This is what he says:

> 'This mound has long been celebrated as the spot on which Henry the Eighth stood to watch the going up of a rocket to assure him that the death of Anne Boleyn would enable him to marry Lady Jane Seymour. This is the tradition of the park, and it has been handed down from father to son by several parkkeepers. There can be no doubt but that this mound

was formerly a British barrow. It has been opened, and a considerable deposit of ashes was found in the centre of it.'

Alas, it is known that Henry VIII spent that evening of 19 May 1536, the day of Anne's execution, in Wiltshire. Euphoria has its limits and a 60-mile ride surely exceeds them, even for a man just freed of a troublesome wife. But it makes a good story, and the name is at least 250 years old and possibly older. In 1637 it was called 'the King's Standing', and may have been a vantage point for falconry in the valley below (on the enclosure map, p.64, one can see 'the Warren', indicating a small royal game reserve below the mound). But Jesse was almost certainly right in identifying it as a prehistoric burial mound, although at some stage it lost its conical top and had been extensively remodelled.

The first (Neolithic) cultivators probably arrived in Britain in about 3500BC. They were apparently the first people to keep animals, for example pigs, and to use a light wooden plough, skills they brought from continental Europe. They did not yet live in villages, but in scattered individual homesteads, small rectangular houses made of wattle (interlaced branches, probably hazel) and daub (a mixture of animal dung and straw), roofed with turf or rushes. Before then humans had lived by hunting and foraging.

It was the people of this new farming culture that first constructed barrows in which to bury their dead. The suspected barrows in the park date any time from about 3000BC to the period when barrow construction petered out, around 900BC. This may seem very imprecise, but the archaeological evidence has been largely destroyed.

We do know, however, without any doubt at all that at least one Late Bronze Age settlement existed in the park. Pottery shards (c.900BC) have been found in the gravel north of Holly

(Bog) Lodge, just west of the riding ring, and one may expect this settlement to have had predecessors (see p.32). The rabbits that abound there still kick up the occasional small shard.

A telescope is now available to see more of the prospect. Having enjoyed the view across the Thames valley, look in the opposite direction through the 'window'. On a clear day you will see St Paul's Cathedral framed by the cutting through Sidmouth Wood. The avenue of sweet chestnuts running up to the cutting marks the alignment of a circular and probably prehistoric earthwork adjacent to and on the eastern side of the horse ride (100m away – it is noticeable because of the bracken growing in it) and another probable barrow, 'Oliver's Mound', which once stood in the Sidmouth Wood cutting but which was destroyed by gravel diggers in 1834. The skeletons they found at the time are unlikely to have been prehistoric on account of the acidity of the soil. However, the alignment of these three supposedly prehistoric features is striking.

The avenue of trees is itself old by our standards. We may not know what tree species was used, but the avenue certainly existed at the beginning of the eighteenth century, as may be seen on the left side of Knyff's 1708 illustration of Petersham Park (p.77).

(Oliver's Mound was supposedly named after Oliver Cromwell, but he came no closer than Ham, in November 1647, so it is an unlikely explanation.)

Proceed southwards through Pembroke Lodge grounds, passing along the rear of the Lodge itself.

Note the veteran oaks in the grounds of Petersham Lodge. These formed part of 'Berry Grove', which features on the enclosure map (see p.64).

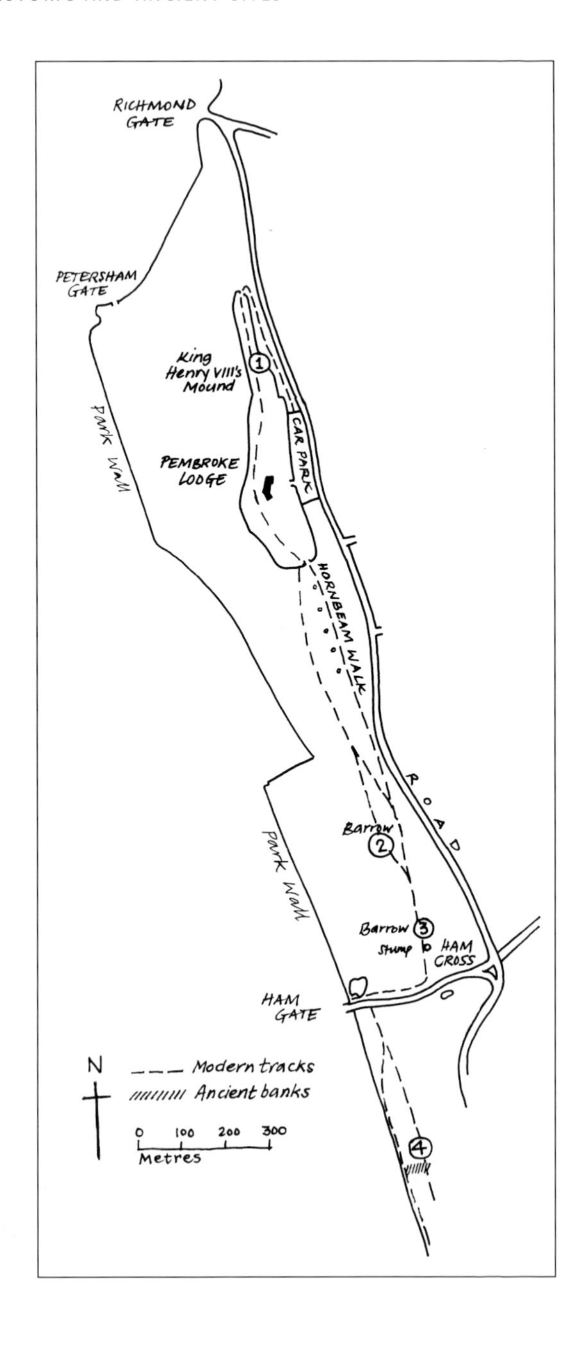
RICHMOND GATE
PETERSHAM GATE
King Henry VIII's Mound
1
Park Wall
PEMBROKE LODGE
CAR PARK
HORNBEAM WALK
ROAD
Barrow
2
Park Wall
Barrow
3
Stump
HAM CROSS
HAM GATE
4
N
Modern tracks
Ancient banks
0 100 200 300
Metres

Keep going straight to leave the Lodge grounds at the wicket gate at the southernmost end of the grounds. Walk along the informal footpath that follows the escarpment (you will notice the more formal Hornbeam Walk running parallel on your left) for approximately 600m. Do not stray from the escarpment edge.

Walking along the escarpment is a good moment to consider the dramatic changes that happened to the landscape of the park in prehistoric times as a result of climate and geology. We are speaking of an enormous time span, for human interest starts almost half a million years ago.

The underlying geological structure of the park is predominantly London Clay but with three main bands of sandy/ gravelly deposits forming high ground, most obviously the escarpment from Richmond Gate to Kingston Hill which you are now following; and also the area north of Holly (Bog) Lodge to East Sheen Gate, the high ground around White Lodge - Spanker's Hill - the Isabella Plantation, and the north west side of the Pen Ponds.

It was during the warmer interglacial phases that early hominids found Britain relatively tolerable and lived here. Virtually all prehistoric artefacts found in the park have, predictably, been found on the gravel terraces left by fluvio-glacial action, not on the clay. At the time of Boxgrove Man, 500,000 years ago, the climate seems to have been warmer than today, with lions and rhinoceroses roaming the landscape. After the next ice age, a period from approximately 470,000 to 430,000 years ago, the climate was often as inhospitable as that today in the Arctic Circle, with a similar tundra landscape. Consequently, humans inhabited the warmer drier sandy gravel areas in preference to the lower, wetter clay areas.

The oldest artefacts found in the park (on high ground near the White Lodge) are flint tools of the Paleolithic period, about 400,000 years ago, during the Great Interglacial Period. They probably belonged to *Homo erectus,* an early hominid predator, thought to be our direct ancestor. During the next interglacial period, 150,000 years ago, fallow deer roamed Britain before disappearing with the last ice age.

More recent flints from the Mesolithic period, that is the period between the end of the last ice age about 8300BC and before the introduction of farming in about 3500BC, have been found at a lower level, around Ham Dip, Dann's Pond and the Pen Ponds. In 1953 a fine flint axe of about 5000-4000BC was found in the Isabella Plantation, and is now on display in the Richmond Museum. These implements belonged to modern humankind *(Homo sapiens sapiens).*

For the first time we can imagine the scene. From about 8000BC the climate was as warm as today, for a short while warmer. The open tundra had given way to trees. The landscape and flora of the park by now were probably recognizably similar to today. First came birch (still present in the park), then pine, hazel and eventually forests, mainly oak but also with elm and lime trees. The animal population changed. Wild horses, mammoth, elk and bison declined or disappeared either as a result of climate change or human predation and were replaced by more familiar woodland animals: red deer, wild ox, boar, badgers, foxes and hedgehogs. People hunted them with flint-tipped spears, and killed and skinned them with flint knives and scrapers.

In about 6500BC, during this Mesolithic period, the land link with the continent was submerged (thank heavens, an island race at last). By now wood was a central material of human culture, used to make axe hafts, harpoon and spear shafts, and also wattle fencing, no doubt very similar to that still used today. They presumably knew about coppicing (see pp.21-22). They had also learnt how to use antler and bone as tools. (So had Boxgrove Man half a million years earlier, but it is unclear whether intervening hominid species had these skills.)

When you have walked about 500m from Pembroke Lodge grounds the path dips and then rises, you should see a large-trunked oak pollard 20 paces on your left, known as John Martin's oak (after a 19th century romantic artist who painted it), standing on what is probably a small prehistoric mound. The tree is worth inspecting since the trunk is more massive than it initially seems. Like the other oak pollards in the park, it is pre-enclosure. Resume the path and you will see that it rises over a distinct mound with an oak growing out of it about 40m ahead.

This is probably a barrow **(2)**. It was excavated in the early nineteenth century, and according to Jesse, broken pottery and ash deposits found. The pottery might have told us the approximate date of the barrow. When one bears in mind the amount of work involved in the construction of barrows it is difficult to believe that they are simply graves in the modern sense. Almost certainly they also held symbolic power, possibly representing the power of dead ancestors, and possibly used as focal points for social, political or economic transactions.

Another possible barrow **(3)**, easy to locate but very much more difficult to spot lies 300m south, and is lost in the bracken except during January-April. To find it continue the same path until you are about 20 paces from a large 6' tall oak stump marking the end of the path. The suspected barrow is on your right, identifiable by two hawthorns and an oak growing on top of it. However, one must be cautious. Barrow **(2)** has already been ruined by excavation. Barrow **(3)** might tell us for sure who constructed them or when. But it would have to compete against other claims on archaeological funding, so do not hold your breath.

Descend to Ham Gate and then follow the path running about 40m in from the wall in a southerly (Kingston Gate) direction. Cross the first culvert with wooden rails, and veer off on the small right hand path. Cross another drainage ditch which exits through a grating in the park wall, and shortly thereafter, where the path almost touches the park wall, you find yourself crossing a dip and a bank (8m wide x 0.5m high) that runs out from the park wall at a right angle.

In his *Monumenta Britannica,* John Aubrey, the seventeenth century antiquarian, noted that

> 'In Ham-heath runs a straight Rampire from the [Richmond] Parke towards the Thames, having the graffe [trench] westwards: it is likely this was made as an obstacle to the Romans; I find several such in the west of England....'

It has never been formally identified but in his 1992 survey, Tom Greeves speculates that this may indeed be the end of Aubrey's 'Rampire' **(4)**. One can see there is a 'graffe' on its west side and the bank seems to be the beginning of a more dramatic dyke now forming a path which runs across Ham Common almost parallel with Church Rd (and may be joined opposite the entrance to Wilmer House, where maintenance of the path has clearly modified it). It probably belongs to the late Iron Age (150BC-43AD) when iron tipped ploughs made the richer but heavier clay soils manageable for the first time, and so brought human settlements down off the gravel plateaux. Perhaps it is the delineation of a field system, it may have been an access causeway to the Thames across marshy ground, since fish would have been a major food source for any settlement near the river.

Resume the main path (about 75m in from the wall) towards Kingston Gate. When the path rises over a shoulder of higher ground you should see on top of the escarpment the unmistakable silhouette of a clump of Scots pine trees above the deciduous trees. This is King's Clump ((5) on the map on p.53). Make for it. It stands almost directly above Gallows Pond. (This mid-nineteenth century pond is named after 'Gallows', the coppice that formed part of Kingston Common in the seventeenth century (Walk No.3), which itself was named after the gallows that stood just outside the park wall).

King's Clump seems to be a well-defined barrow. It is noteworthy that all these probable barrows, with the exception of Oliver's Mound, are sited on the very edge of the Thames valley escarpment, commanding the vieoss t oss the valley. It is difficult to escape the conclusion that siting was an important feature of barrow construction. As for the Scots pines, they were planted in the nineteenth century, because their height and distinctive canopy was considered 'scenic'. Scots pines are never natural this far south, but always planted. Until the late eighteenth century Scots pines were usually planted with a purpose. Their high and distinctive profile rendered them ideal as 'signposts' for drovers looking for lodging for the night as they brought their livestock to London. By the nineteenth century however, this practical use had given way to the pine as scenery.

Proceed in a north easterly direction, parallel to the carriageway in the direction of Robin Hood Gate, passing Ladderstile Gate on your right and making for the car park at the top of Broomfield Hill (1.5km). Pass through the car park and begin walking down Broomfield Hill following a footpath that leads straight down the hill as the carriageway curves to

the left. As it descends, the path crosses the remains of two or three concentric banks (6) that more or less follow the curve of the hill around the edge of Broomfield Hill Wood.

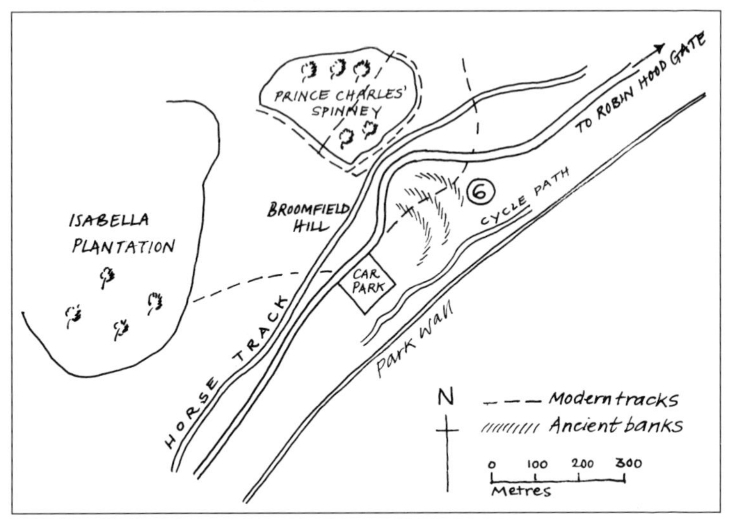

Greeves thinks it is possible that these banks were defensive on purpose. Broomfield Hill lies just over a mile away from the more impressive fort at Caesar's Camp on Wimbledon Common with which, without the tree cover, it would have been in sight. Hill forts became common during the Iron Age, from 500BC until 150BC when their construction declined. Incidentally, Aubrey remarked on Caesar's Camp: 'It is certain that this fortification was built by the Danes.... methinks they are too artish for the old Britons.' What does the fellow mean, too *artish?*

The quickest way back to Pembroke Lodge is to skirt the north east side of Isabella plantation and cross Pond Slade, making for White Ash Lodge, Oak Lodge and thence to Pembroke Lodge (2.5km).

(At the outset of this journey you may care to explore the cutting through Prince Charles' Spinney, which is strewn with bluebells and daffodils in spring. A few hawthorns more or less justify its name, but this grove is mainly composed of other tree cover.)

AFTERWORD

Another suspected and possibly important prehistoric site, identified by Greeves, lies in the southern part of Sidmouth Wood and is inaccessible to the public. Two parallel banks, about 40m apart, with ditches on the outside, extend for just over 300m. He speculates that these might be part of a *cursus,* a ritual structure of the third millennium BC. One reason for his thinking that they are probably prehistoric in age is that there is no evidence of any agricultural activity in this part of the park, then part of Petersham Common, before its enclosure in 1637.

The Park in the late Middle Ages

Were we able to see the area that is now the park as it looked in the Middle Ages, we should probably find it unrecognizable. In prehistoric times the wooden plough was not strong enough to turn the richer soils in the valley, so people had preferred to live on the thinner sandy upland soils. With the invention of the iron-tipped plough and the employment of oxen, people abandoned the uplands for the Thames valley. One may therefore guess that part of the park area reverted to woodland, only to be partly cleared again in Saxon times.

Trees and shrub probably grew where now it is open. There was no deer herd, so the 'browse line' would only have existed where livestock were allowed to roam. By the Middle Ages the area was the meeting point of different manorial estates, most notably Mortlake, Petersham and Shene [Richmond].

We know a little about the area from the *Domesday Book* of 1086, with its catalogue of settlements. The area around the park was one of the more populous parts of Surrey, but with perhaps 15 persons per square mile it remained astonishingly sparse compared with today. As for the park area itself, you could have walked it and probably met no one.

The manor was the basic economic and administrative unit for the countryside and an essential foundation of the feudal system. The manorial lords were the ruling elite, vassals of the king or princes of the church, holding their lands courtesy of Crown or Church. The ordinary manor tenants, except for a minority of 'freemen', were physically bound to the manor, unable to leave the land or their duty of servitude. It was they, the peasantry, who underpinned both the feudal and ecclesiastical structures.

Almost half of what became the park fell within the manor of Mortlake, held by the archbishops of Canterbury until the Reformation. Mortlake originally extended as far as (and included) Wimbledon, which later became a manor in its own right. Manors had a tendency to create sub-manors which over time became independent entities. Petersham was held by the Abbot of Chertsey. The manor of Kingston originally stretched to Kew and included the lands of the manor of Shene (known as Richmond from 1501), which had become a separate manor by 1130. By the thirteenth century, the middle of the park in the area around the White Lodge and Spanker's Hill, constituted a very small manorial estate, Hartington Combe, wedged between Mortlake and Petersham manors. It was held by Merton Priory, second only to Southwark among the great religious foundations of Surrey.

Manorial land fell into two administrative categories, that for the sole benefit of the manor lord, the 'demesne' land, and that allocated for the benefit of the tenants, the 'common' land. We can be fairly sure that most of the land in the park area was common land, simply because it represented the poorest lands of each manor. The demesne would have the lion's share of the best land, the pick of the valley lands, which boasted the richest soils. Manors usually possessed four types of land: arable, pasture and meadow, woodland and finally 'waste' land. The pasture and meadow were principally near the riverbank, areas that tended to be either frequently inundated as flood meadow or lands a little further inland which were still moist. The best arable land would be in the river valley also. One can safely speculate that most of what is now the park was common 'waste', open heath, scrub, waterlogged tracts and woodland, its usefulness described on pp.23-26. The steward of the manor would ensure an equitable and controlled allocation of the waste's resources.

However, traces on the landscape indicate that some areas within what became the park were indeed brought under the plough during the middle ages, probably in the period 1150-1250 when, as a result of population growth, the extent of village arable land doubled all over England as waste lands were reclaimed. Some of the major boundary banks and ditches that can still be found in the park were probably dug in this period.

The map drawn by Nicholas Lane between 1632 and 1637 (pp.64-66) indicates what the park wall would enclose. While we do not know how old the details on this map are, the probability is that many of the field boundaries and roads date back into the Middle Ages. One reason for this assumption is that some oaks, approximately 500-700 years old, still survive in the park, some indicating old hedgerow lines, others marking parish or manorial boundaries. Although Lane's map contains inaccuracies, it still provides an insight into what preceded the park. Lane marks more fields in private tenure than was likely to have been the case in the late Middle Ages, but he still shows the manorial common lands, one of Mortlake's common open fields 'Upper Town Field', and marks coppices and hayfields, the former vital for wooden tools, the latter as the only winter feed for livestock.

There are three principal medieval features in the park: 'ridge and furrow' ploughing; banks, ditches or ancient oak pollards which are vestiges of field boundaries; and roads. Two routes ran through the park, one from Mortlake to Ham (which entered the park at the west end of Teck Plantation (west of East Sheen Gate) and the other from Shene (Richmond Gate) to Coombe (Ladderstile Gate). They intersected at Ham Cross. There were also access roads to farmland, notably to Hartleton (as Hartington became known by the seventeenth century) farm, and Hill Farm.

The north east section of the Park

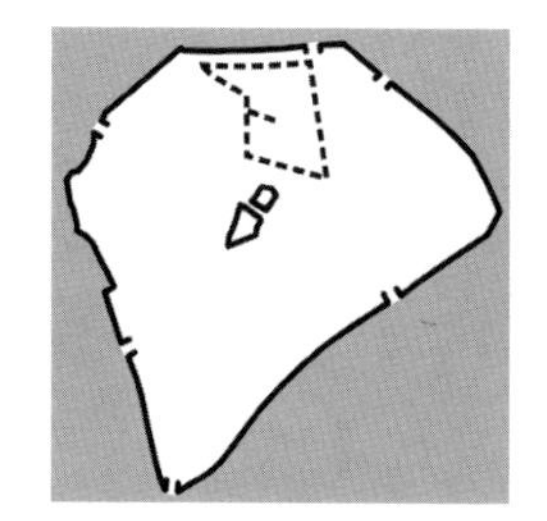

Distance 5km: 2 hours

(On which one may see medieval field boundaries, ridge and furrow plough marks and a section of the Mortlake-Ham highway.)

ONLY UNDERTAKE THIS WALK BETWEEN MID-DECEMBER AND MAY WHEN GROUND COVER IS MINIMAL. SOME FEATURES ARE DIFFICULT TO SPOT. DO NOT SPOIL YOUR WALK HUNTING TOO LONG FOR THEM. YOU MAY NOTICE THEM ANOTHER TIME WHEN YOU WALK THAT WAY.

Start: Go to Bog Gate (closest car park at East Sheen Gate) and walk 100m to the south east corner of the metal fenced enclosure adjoining the park wall to the west of Bog Gate.

This is the intersection of what are probably the western and northern boundaries **(7)** of Hill Farm, see map on p.42. The western boundary of Hill Farm is the distinct ditch and bank following the line of an unsurfaced path (parallel and 50m west of the gravel path leading from Bog Gate).

Follow it and cross the horse ride and continue to follow it till it peters out. Another 60 paces brings you to a line of ancient oaks (8) on a barely discernible bank, running NW-SE towards Holly (Bog) Lodge.

These oaks are medieval, 600 or even 700 years old, and were once part of a hedgerow. Another very incomplete line of ancient trees runs southwards from your right towards the small pond on the east side of Conduit Wood. This possibly marked the south west side of Hill Farm **(9)**.

Return towards the intersection of the northern and western boundaries of Hill Farm, but go to the north-east corner of the Riding Ring.

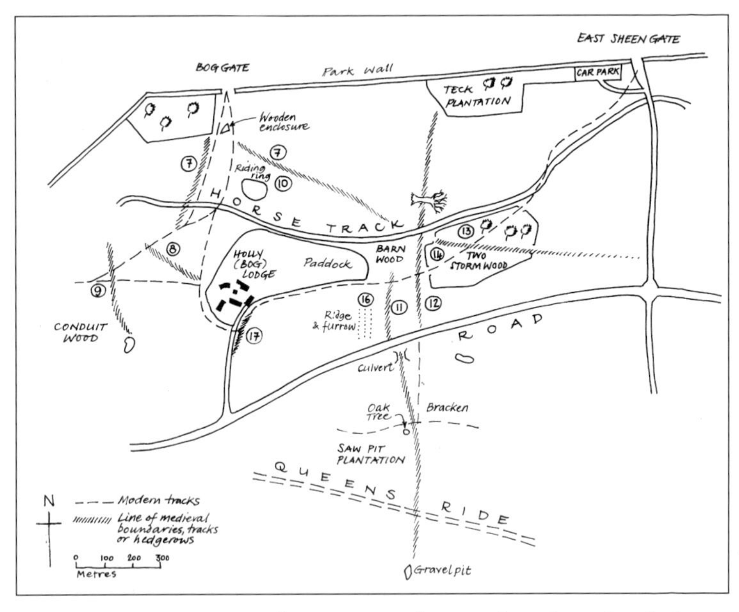

From here you may see that you are close to the edge of a slight bank (50 paces north) running from the corner of the metal fencing enclosure roughly SE towards the northern edge of Barn Wood. This is the northern boundary of Hill Farm, and the edge of the access track **(7)**, or worple way, running along the northern edge of the farm marked on Lane's map (p.64). Hill Farm homestead **(10)** stood near the edge of the bank, but it is unclear whether it was standing there in the middle ages.

Follow the line of the bank (Hill Farm track) to the northern edge of Barn Wood.

If you consult Lane's map you will see that this is where Hill Field abutted Deane's Lane (**11** and **12**). Deane's Lane was an integral part of the road from Mortlake to Ham. This road runs from the kink in the west edge of Teck Plantation, where one can still see a slight depression by a lone oak tree, southwards to about 20 metres west of the north-west corner of the fencing of Two Storm Wood. On Lane's map the highway ran along the border between Little Heathe and Longe Lande. It was still in use in the mid-eighteenth century, as can be seen on Eyre's map (p.87).

According to Greeves, a wooden building stood at this intersection, at the indent of the Two Storm Wood metal fencing close to the NW gate (currently locked), see map on p.44. It must have been a rudimentary, timber-framed structure with walls of thin wattle (interlaced coppiced wood, or tree shoots) and daub (dung and straw), its roof made of turf or thatch. The floor would have been earth, strewn with rushes. Stone or brick floors only came to be used by the peasantry in the late middle ages. The timber base would have eventually rotted in the ground and it had probably collapsed by Lane's time. Later buildings had padstones or a stone or brick course to keep the wooden base off the ground. Wattle and daub was a very effective building material, so long as the timber frame was strong. However, it was progressively displaced in the seventeenth century by brick or stone, and unfairly dismissed, in the words of one contemporary, as little more than 'paper work', though it is still standing and doing fine in many parts of the country.

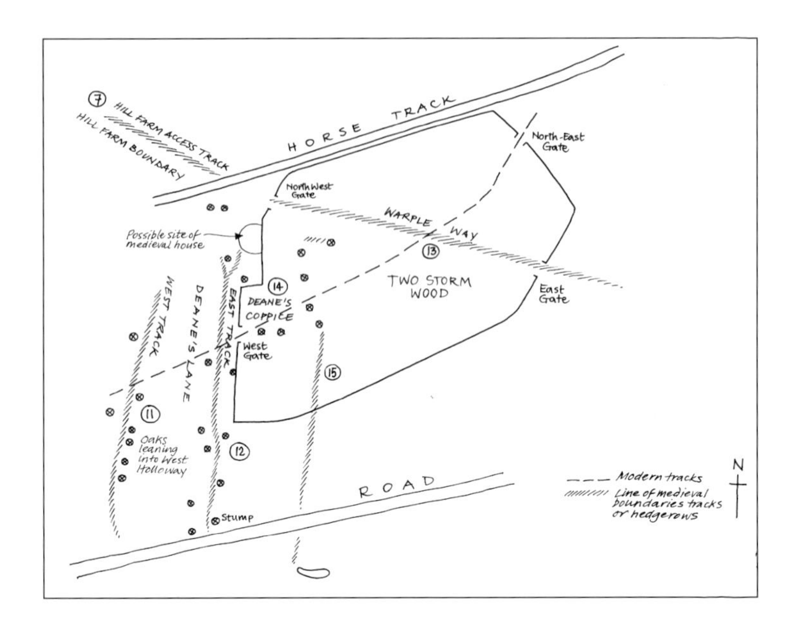

This building stood at the crossroads between Deane's Lane, and the warple way from Hill Farm, which continues eastwards (**13**), across Two Storm Wood more or less as far as the carriageway to East Sheen Gate.

Enter Two Storm Wood by the west gate.

This was Deane's Coppice (**14**) The west side is lined by the metal fence. You will be immediately aware of the magnificent ancient oaks, which probably already stood over the coppice 400 years ago. Coppiced wood was an essential feature of any village in the Middle Ages to provide the basic artefacts of life (on coppice, see p.21-22). A slight bank runs down the east side of the coppice (**15**), towards the carriageway, most easily discernible from near Barn Wood Pond on the far side of the carriageway.

As you cross Two Storm Wood you will cross the warple way, slightly sunken, each end marked by a metal gate (on the north-west and east sides of the perimeter fence). It continues eastwards (but from the wood it is invisible) across the open ground (to the East Sheen carriageway). (It can be discerned as a slight bank running across the greensward if one stands on the Richmond-Roehampton carriageway, close to Sheen Cross.) On Lane's map the warple way divided Longe Lande and Bittin Furlongs in the Mortlake Upper Town Field.

Retrace your steps to the west gate of Two Storm Wood.

Deane's Lane still has two quite distinct 'hollow ways' or sunken lanes running, running more or less parallel, one presumably abandoned at some point in favour of the other. The eastern track (**12**) runs just a few paces outside the western boundary fence of Two Storm Wood.

The western track of Deane's Lane (11) is the easier to follow. It lies 75 paces or so west of the west edge of Two Storm Wood.

It is most easily observable at the southern end, close to the Richmond-Roehampton carriageway where the ground is boggy and the oaks tend to lean inwards, from the old banks into the sunken lane. One may speculate that the existence of two tracks here indicates one was abandoned in favour of a new track, presumably because the former became waterlogged and impassable for carts.

Before proceeding towards Ham along the holloway, the south-west part of Barn Wood (west of Deane's Lane) is a good area for observing ridge and furrow plough marks, running north-south. Ridge and furrow is a subtle feature and difficult to spot. You may have to get close to the ground to see the 'ripple' of the furrows or walk slowly westwards, parallel to the carriage way, to the west edge of Barn Wood and you should notice you are crossing regular undulations, like corrugation, roughly 12 paces apart.

A brief background to ridge and furrow may be helpful. The Saxons introduced an 'open field' system of farming. Within the village each household might be expected to hold a certain number of strips of the common open fields, of which there might be three or four, very large by our standards, each containing perhaps 100 acres. The demesne land would have similar fields, for the benefit of the lord. Each field would usually follow an annual cycle to produce a winter crop, for example wheat or rye, in the first year and a spring crop, barley or oats, in the second. In the third year it lay fallow and livestock grazed on it. Each tenant would be assigned strips, or 'selions', in each field as was his due. The steward would keep a tally of the land rights and also duties of each tenant family. Duty would mean the completion of a certain number of days' service tending the demesne land.

The land was apportioned in strips to make ploughing more efficient. Because a yoke of oxen was difficult to turn, it made sense to minimise how often the plough had to be turned. In theory each strip was one 'furrow long' or furlong (220 yards) in length, but there were inevitably variations. The general intention was to plough a distance until the oxen required a breather, and then to turn the plough. The plough threw earth to the right, and the ploughman would start at the centre and work his way clockwise outwards. There were two virtues to this procedure. First, the ridge ran along the centre of a selion and the furrows marked a clear border between one selion and another. More importantly it allowed the water to run off. Good drainage was essential. For that reason also, ridge and furrow invariably ran with the slope of the hill rather than across it.

Ploughing was a task that demanded skill and a patient temperament, as one thirteenth century text states:

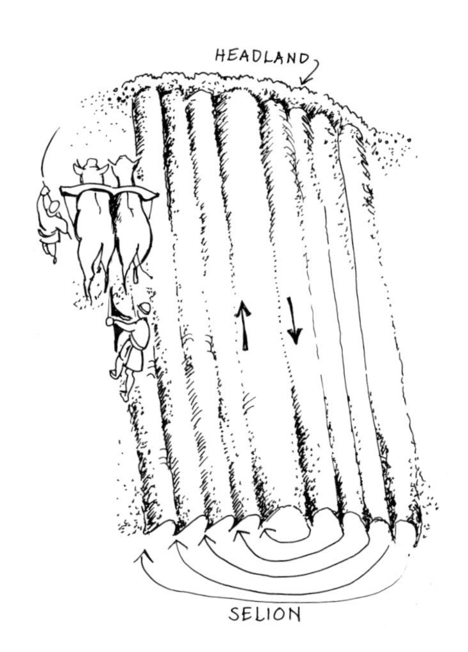

> 'The art of the ploughman consists in knowing how to draw a straight furrow with yoked oxen without striking, pricking or ill-treating them. Ploughmen should be neither melancholy nor irritable but gay and joyful and encourage the oxen with melody and song.... They ought to be so attached to them that they sleep in their stable at night....'

A moment of self-knowledge is in order. In my case, the furrows would have been crooked and both my oxen and myself frustrated and extremely cross.

The width between furrows varies from one era to another. The wider they are, the older they are likely to be. The widest (12m) and probably oldest (possibly Saxon, and in the gift of Chertsey Abbey) are on low ground beside Ham Gate. The furrows in Barn Wood are approximately 9m wide. Later, yet narrower furrows reflect improved ploughing technology which required fewer oxen.

This particular arable seems to have been abandoned in, or after, the fourteenth century and planted with oaks. It is identified on Lane's Map as 'Hill Coppice' (**16**). Why was the old field abandoned? We may only speculate. During the late thirteenth and early fourteenth centuries the English economy expanded rapidly with increasing demand for timber and fuel. We know for example that the Abbot of Chertsey, 1307-46, who held Petersham manor, was assiduous in thickening and planting woods. However, there is also another more probable reason. In the years 1290-1375 Britain entered a phase of chronic climatic instability. The years 1315-22 were particularly bad with ruined harvests, famine and rocketing prices. By 1320 the population was already in decline. By 1340 there was already a corresponding decline in cultivation. Then came the knock-out blow. In 1348-9 the Black Death killed over one third of the population and land all over Europe went out of production. This land was the poorest and farthest land from Mortlake village. With such a drastic reduction in labour it would have made sense to turn this land over to timber and wood production, valuable commodities which required less labour. If it had not happened in the first four decades of this disastrous century, it must have happened in the fifth.

Beyond the open fields system lay the common pasturage, usually the poorest waste ground on which manorial tenants could graze livestock, or gather wood, furze for kindling, heather and bracken for litter, rushes and turf.

Across the greensward beyond Barn Wood, the approach road to Holly (Bog) Lodge crosses the western edge of Adder Downe (**17**), marked on Lane's map. It is readily visible, marked by a slight bank and a row of oak trees. It is marked on the sketch map for this walk and you may care to note it when you next pass that way. 'Adder' probably refers to the vipers here, now sadly lost, probably as a result of human activity.

Return to the west track of Deane's Lane and cross the carriageway.

The western track of Deane's Lane/Mortlake-Ham road (**11**) can be followed across the carriageway where it can be discerned as a slight causeway, presumably over what was boggy ground. The causeway can be located if you look for an (almost buried) brick culvert under the causeway, about 30 paces from the carriageway. After another 15 paces, note an old oak tree on your left, and you will observe it stands on a very low bank running to Barn Wood Pond.

This is probably the southern boundary of Deane's Coppice.

Continue walking up the causeway, running well nigh straight up the hill to Saw Pit Plantation more or less along the line of the path entering the bracken towards the top of the hill, slightly on the left of the path.

Sawpits fell into abeyance during the course of the nineteenth century. They were used to cut tree trunks lengthways, for floorboards. The tree would be felled green and flawed, and the trunk roughly squared off with an adze. This made it safer since it could not roll. The trunk would be placed on two cross pieces over the top of the sawpit. Two men, one standing above the trunk and one in the pit were required to operate the saw. The man in the pit did most of the hard work, the teeth cutting during the downward pull. The man above was responsible for ensuring it cut in a straight line.

Enter Saw Pit Plantation on the path, and about fifteen paces to your left you should locate the holloway, a very slight trough in the ground, running almost parallel with the path. It is quite difficult to locate, but it remains quite close to, and left of, the path across the plantation to Queen's Ride, although it is obstructed by one or two fallen trees. If you find parts of it, your faith will be vindicated when you cross the Queen's Ride where the remains of the holloway is visible as a ripple in the Ride. The holloway is finally lost in the flooded gravel pit the far side of the Queen's Ride.

Walk down the Queen's Ride to the White Lodge.

Here you can locate perhaps the most obvious example of ridge and furrow in the whole park, on the triangle of ground surrounded by tarmac carriageways just south of the White Lodge. the furrows running east-west. Other good examples may be found north of the White Lodge or in Duchess Wood north west of the White Lodge. in both cases the furrows running west-east. In these two cases cultivation was abandoned and the land wooded.

Return to East Sheen Gate following the road from the White Lodge (1.3km).

Lane's map indicates that the tarmac carriageway approximately overlays the access road which served Hartleton Farm (as Hartington manor became known by the seventeenth century).

The south west section of the Park

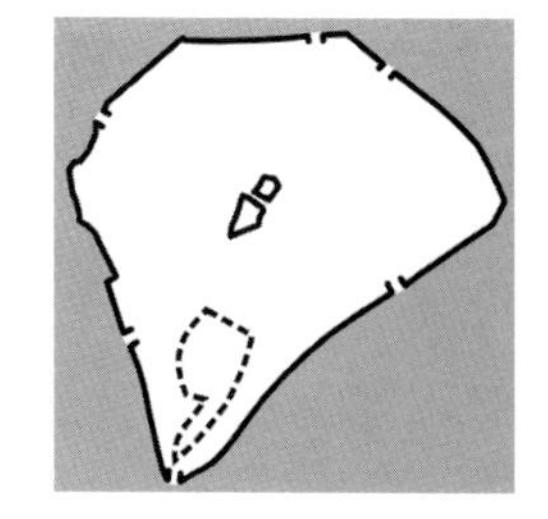

Distance 3km: 1 hour

DO NOT ATTEMPT THIS WALK EXCEPT BETWEEN MID-DECEMBER AND MAY WHEN GROUND COVER IS MINIMAL. SOME FEATURES ARE DIFFICULT TO SPOT.

The final and most impressive section of the medieval Shene (Richmond) - Coombe highway (**18**) merits a visit on its own (see map on p.53). It will be recalled from the introduction to the park in the late middle ages, that this highway crossed the Mortlake-Ham road at Ham Cross, and ran to Ladderstile Gate, its traces now petering out near Dann's Pond. In the 1630s it was bounded by Lambert Hawes on its western side, and Nine Acres, Sixteen Acres and Blacke Heathe on its eastern side (see enclosure map, p.66). How old these names are, we cannot say. Field names can easily change from one generation to another, but for a discussion of their meanings, see pp.62-68.

Start at the Kingston Gate car park. Cross the road. Ahead you will see a track running across the greensward towards Gallows Pond. However, turn right and follow the path running uphill into the trees close to the road up Kingston Hill. Stop at the tree line and find the bank running northwards more or less along the tree line (19).

This is the western boundary of 'Gallows', clearly marked on Lane's map. ('Gallows' is probably a reference to the gallows that stood just outside the present Kingston Gate.) If you follow this bank, you may notice a kink, the beginning of a ditch running off to the left (westwards). This appears to be the boundary between Little Common Field and Hare Snatch on the enclosure map.

Continue along the boundary bank of Gallows.

It brings you down to Gallows Pond, through the Sugar Maple plantation (see p.171), roughly where the northern edge of Hare Snatch seems to have been. Looking down the gully, the edge of Hare Snatch, two tall oak trees may be seen just the far side of the carriageway. These seem to mark the continuing boundary of Hare Snatch.

Follow the path past Gallows Pond.

The beginning of the 'bulge' marked on Lane's map as the border of the next field with Gallows seems to run out from the pond across your path and into the trees, but it is difficult to follow.

Proceed up the path to Thatched House Lodge. When you reach the tarmac you will see two informal paths running off to your right in a northerly direction. Take the right hand path that runs to the left of Coronation Plantation. After 50m you reach a large oak tree on your left and four others on your right. Follow the slight ditch running off to the left for 30 paces to the rotting remains of a tree, which lies at the head of a depression. Follow the depression running parallel with the path you have just left.

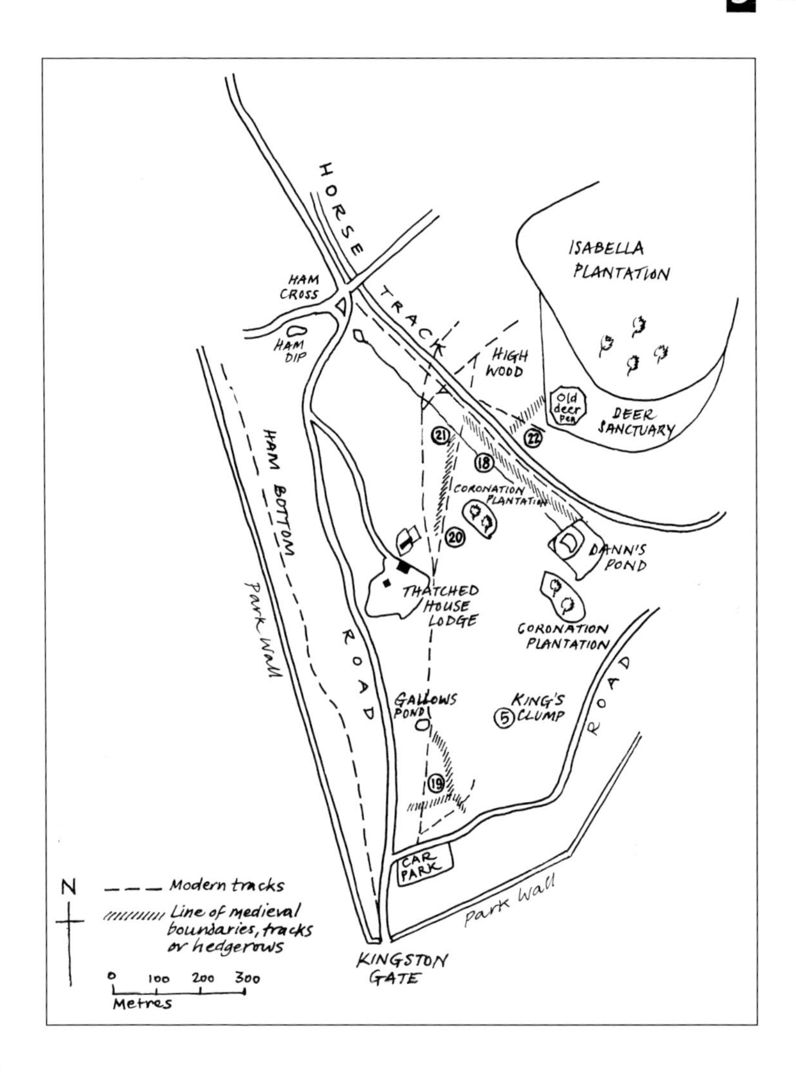
HORSE TRACK
HAM CROSS
HAM DIP
ISABELLA PLANTATION
HIGH WOOD
Old deer pen
DEER SANCTUARY
HAM BOTTOM
Park Wall
CORONATION PLANTATION
DANN'S POND
THATCHED HOUSE LODGE
CORONATION PLANTATION
ROAD
GALLOWS POND
KING'S CLUMP
ROAD
CAR PARK
Park Wall
KINGSTON GATE
N
Modern tracks
Line of medieval boundaries, tracks or hedgerows
0 100 200 300
Metres

This is a medieval field boundary (**20**). It had ceased to be a boundary by 1632 since it is not marked on Lane's enclosure map.

Just before the boundary ditch plunges into the stream note on your left broken ground with a circular earthwork (21).

Greeves believes this was some kind of medieval enclosure, possibly for folding sheep. Given the name of the field in 1637, Lambert Hawes (see p.68), this fold may have been connected with lambing each spring. Sheep were far smaller than now. Before the selective breeding of the eighteenth century the average sheep weighed only 20kg compared with 90kg today.

Cross the stream and follow the path up the far side. Just before you reach the junction with another footpath and the horsetrack, note the depression in the bracken on your right. This is the Shene-Coombe highway (18). Follow it for 120 paces. Then climb up to the horse track and you should see a bank and ditch (22) running at a right angle into High Wood.

This bank marks the boundary hedgerow between Sixteen Acres and Black Heath, both on Lane's map. The older oak pollards to be found on the Black Heath (now part of High Wood) are at least 600 years old, some of them possibly more, and may be the remains of medieval wood pasture.

Return to, and continue up the Shene-Coombe highway to Dann's Pond (enclosed by fencing and trees), where it peters out. Proceed around Dann's Pond in a clockwise direction and return to Kingston Gate car park.

AFTERWORD

One other major medieval feature should be noted. Although Beverley Brook, which runs across the eastern side of the park, has been straightened and embanked in recent times, its name testifies to its early medieval origins: 'Beaver stream' ('ley' is the corrupted form of *lacu:* Anglo Saxon for stream). Beavers became extinct in England in the eleventh or twelfth century and the name presumably predates this. The brook formed a manorial boundary (see p.147). With its straightening, the borough boundary wanders apparently aimlessly from one side of the brook to the other. Where possible medieval boundaries followed natural features. Even if the brook wandered, there could be no argument. The brook defined the boundary. By straightening one also speeds up a brook that *wants* to meander and wants to aggregate to itself a far richer habitat for flora and fauna. Our control freakery can be so bad for the natural world.

The enclosure of Richmond Park in the seventeenth century

THE STORY OF ENCLOSURE

Richmond Park is really a misnomer. Until its enclosure in 1637 the park comprised lands belonging mainly to the parishes, which had replaced the manorial system as the smallest administrative unit during the Tudor period. These were: Ham (895 acres), Mortlake (732 acres), Petersham (306 acres) and Roehampton (200 acres). Kingston, Richmond and Putney lands constituted 117, 69 and 36 acres respectively. The park acquired its name through its association with the royal palace of Richmond.

Gravel uplands made poor arable land but excellent hunting country, and Charles I began to covet it for his own pleasure. (In this he was merely following a pattern established by the Normans in designating as forest, tracts of poor land on which to indulge their love of hunting.) In the words of a contemporary, Edward Hyde, Earl of Clarendon, in his History of the Rebellion and the Civil Wars of England:

> 'The King, who was excessively affected to Hunting, and the Sports of the Field, had a great desire to make a great Park for Red, as well as Fallow Deer, between Richmond and Hampton Court where he had large Wasts of his own and great parcels of Wood.'

He wanted something larger than the hunting parks of his predecessors, notably the 370 acre park beside the Richmond Palace on the riverbank created by his father, James I (described in *The Thames from Richmond to Putney Bridge*). Yet, as Clarendon pointed out,

'...some Parishes had Commons in those Wasts, so, many Gentlemen, and Farmers, had good Houses, and good Farms intermingled with those Wasts of their own Inheritance, or for their Lives, or Years; and without taking of Them into the Park, it would not be of the largeness, or for the use proposed.'

Lane's map, probably surveyed in 1632 (or even earlier) but finalised in January 1637, showed how many landholders the King had to deal with. It also reveals through field names something of the character of the area.

Basically four kinds of lands were involved: privately held lands, demesne (or manorial) lands that were leased out, manorial open fields and common land, mainly pasturage, for the benefit of the tenants. Some holdings were substantial, for example Henry White's Hill Farm in the northwest part of Mortlake; others held plots of land in more than one parish, most notably Gregory Cole who had inherited from his father substantial holdings in the manors of Ham and Petersham and also at Hartleton Farm, originally a separate manor belonging to Merton Priory.

Clarendon continues:

'... his Majesty desired to purchase these lands and was very willing to buy them upon higher terms than the people could sell them at to anybody else, and thought it no unreasonable thing upon those terms to expect from his subjects.'

In December 1634 Charles began negotiations to purchase the properties in his proposed 'New Park'. Anyone who has watched a large corporation squeezing smallholders so as to enlarge its own landholding will not be surprised that:

'The major part of the people were in a short time prevailed with, but many obstinately refused and it made a great noise as if the King would take away men's estates at his own pleasure.'

None of us like being bullied, not even with fistfuls of money, and it was not long before Charles' unpopularity spread beyond the affected parishes:

'...it was too near London not to be the common discourse.'

Both the Lord Treasurer and the Chancellor of the Exchequer vainly sought to dissuade him from making himself so needlessly unpopular.

The following April, when he had secured barely five acres, he ordered the construction of a nine foot high wall around the whole area he coveted, the bricks being made on site. It was completed in less than three years, but there was difficulty in assembling a sufficient local workforce, possibly because the whole enterprise was so unpopular. At any rate, instructions were issued early in 1636 to 'all Mayors and others the King's officers' to assist him 'in taking up the required bricklayers, labourers, carts and carriages'. But the wall was built too hastily. It required extensive repairs over the next 25 years.

With the wall being built before their very eyes, most land holders reluctantly came to terms, accepting the king's compulsory generosity with as good a grace as could be mustered. Those who refused to treat lost their land anyway.

NICHOLAS LANE'S ENCLOSURE MAP

Lane produced his enclosure map in order to calculate the amount of compensation due to each landholder. It tells us an enormous amount about the landscape in the early seventeenth century. In this we are extremely fortunate, for there are very few places where such a detailed land-holding map of this period has survived and nowhere else in the Greater London area where one may compare a detailed map of this age with a still open landscape.

One must be impressed by the quality of the 1637 survey (which may be consulted in the National Archives). It may contain factual errors but the survey itself is mostly very close to the physical traces which survive to the present. However, the superimposition of Lane's map onto a modern sketch map reveals some distortions. These have required a small amount of fudging. This is particularly so in the northern area between Richmond Gate and East Sheen Gate, where Lane's survey seems to have gone astray. Lane demarcates Richmond parish as a deep wedge into the park. Yet the boundary probably always followed the stream that flows from Sidmouth Wood down through Conduit Wood to the edge of the park close to Richmond Cemetery. We know this stream was the boundary in more recent times and there seems no documentary evidence to show it has ever been changed. Mortlake's boundary with what became the Manor of Richmond was almost certainly established before the Norman Conquest. The Saxons preferred physically obvious boundaries: a stream, river, watershed or some other natural feature over which there could be no dispute. So Lane's delineation has been amended to conform with the route of the stream on the redrawn map here. One may suspect that Lane was a little cavalier in this part of the proposed park, since this area was so poor it was all common waste, without any enclosures and therefore with minimal financial implication. Another area of fudge concerns Hill Farm, where the surviving physical ditches and banks do not quite accord with where Lane has placed them on his map. The dotted lines on the redrawn map indicate manorial boundaries, with Hartleton (once Hartington) Farm being an outpost of Merton Priory, dissolved c.1539.

Two further caveats are in order. There are still today a substantial number of ancient oaks which were standing in 1637, some of which undoubtedly indicate old boundaries or hedgerow lines. Tracing all these and pondering how, if at all, they corroborate or modify Lane's survey is a major exercise that still requires to be done. This may vindicate Lane's work where it is currently doubted.

That said, much information can be gleaned simply by scrutinising the re-drawn version of Lane's map superimposed on a simplified sketch map of the park as it is today. I hope that walkers will take particular pleasure in imagining the early seventeenth century landscape through this map. The old highways, partly traced in Walks 2 and 3 can be seen clearly. Trees were not confined to designated woods and coppices. They also grew elsewhere. There were virtually none on Richmond Common, but there was limited tree cover straddling the Ham-Petersham common boundary, and if one now walks Pond Slade, the ancient oaks that must have been there in 1637 are still to be seen. Most notably, there were (and still are) ancient trees on Black Heath (now High Wood).

It is the field names which fascinate. I have replicated the names as they appear on Lane's map, despite their sometimes arch spellings. Some are a mystery. 'Rutnells' probably refers to a previous landholder, of whom we know nothing. One may presume that it dates from the Tudor period, a time when so much land, principally church land, was enclosed for private use. The field term 'close' was used to indicate freshly enclosed land in the Tudor period. We know little or nothing of most of the tenants marked on the map, so I have ignored them. I have only marked with a 'C' or a 'J' those lands held by Gregory Cole and the Juxon family respectively, apart from 'Rex', the few pockets held either directly or sub-let by the Crown. Both the Cole and Juxon families were important landholders and both are of interest. The little we know about Gregory Cole has been mentioned above.

As for the Juxons, they were a well-known London merchant family. The father, John, was a freeman of the Merchant Taylors Company and made a lucrative living as a sugar baker/refiner in Walbrook. On his wife's death he acquired the manor of East Sheen and Westhall in 1619 (the manor house was badly damaged by fire in 2005). He was well connected. His cousin, William, became bishop of London, attended Charles I on the scaffold in 1649 and became archbishop of Canterbury after the time of the Restoration. John Juxon, however, was of a more Puritan stamp than his cousin. When he died in 1626, he left most of his East Sheen estate to his sons, John and Thomas. The loss of land to the king's hunting park weighed far less heavily with them than their strongly held religious convictions. Thomas remained at the heart of the Puritan network in London. Both of them served in the Parliamentarian forces against the Crown. John died of his wounds in battle at Newbury. Thomas survived the civil war. He should not have adopted his motto, *probus invider nemini* (Upright, an envier of no one), for after the Restoration he became an 'Irish adventurer', coveting and acquiring title to extensive lands there.

Of more interest are those names which say something either about the nature of the landscape or how it was being used. Many remain a mystery. Others are too obvious to merit discussion, but a few explanations are listed here:

(i) Coppice and copse indicate enclosures of underwood, but one cannot be absolutely sure they were still coppice nor that all those enclosures called woods actually were still woods.

(ii) Heath was a man-made environment through the use of poor soil as grazing, thereby creating a specific landscape dominated by grasses, sedges, rushes and shrubs like furze or gorse, juniper, broom and heather and attracting specific heath-loving fauna. One tiny clump of heather still remains and testifies to a plant almost certainly much more widespread once, but a victim of trampling and bracken encroachment. Much of the present park must have been a mix of dry and boggy heathland before the enclosure.

GLOSSARY OF FIELD AND FEATURE NAMES

NORTH WEST SECTION

Adder Down: presumably indicates that adders were once here, but now probably rendered extinct, presumably victims of too much human activity. If they are still around, no one seems to have seen one.

The Arbour: an arbour came to mean a summer shelter, a gazebo. But its name origin indicates it was at first simply the shade offered by a clump of trees and this is probably what this one was.

Berry Grove: bere indicates barley, suggesting it may once have been a barley field, but *bearu* means a small wood, exactly the same as *graf* from which 'grove' derives. So it may be a tautology, and this seems more likely given the difficulty over growing barley on such a steep slope, while trees would have helped hold the soil and prevent erosion.

Burnt Close: was probably a recently enclosed area where woodland may have been cleared by burning. The trees would have been 'ring-barked' in winter to prevent the sap rising. Once the trees had died they would be felled for timber. The undergrowth and stumps would have been burnt, leaving soil enriched with potash, useful given the comparative poorness of the soil.

Lord's Coppice: possibly indicated that it was demesne land in what otherwise was land held in common.

Short Thorns indicates an area where thorn trees once grew, possibly as scrub (as implied by 'Short').

Sudbrook: is simply the 'south brook'.

Warren: this had extended quite a way beyond the new park wall. A warren was simply a hunting ground, principally for hares, possibly rabbits if a rabbit warren was maintained there, for other beasts of the field and for falconry. When one considers it in connection with the 'King's Standing', what is now mis-called King Henry VIII's Mound, its purpose may have been an area for falconry, the standing providing a vantage point for watching a bird of prey in action in the valley below.

White Conduit: is a springhead, tapped in 1500 by Henry VII for his palace by the river, with a brick edifice constructed over the spring (see p.80).

NORTH EAST SECTION

Alder Hill: is barely a hill, but is presumably where alders grew, an indication that prior to draining the ground now used for rugby and other sports, this land must once have been very wet, at least along the course of the feeder stream for Beverley Brook.

Ashen Close, is named after ash trees. The Shrew Ash, an ancient ash pollard (see p.168), probably grew on the southern boundary of Ashen Close. The oak pollards on the north and west sides of Adam's Pond may mark the close's north-west corner.

Beverley Brook: is a Saxon name, *beofor-lac*, beaver stream, testimony to the presence of beavers here before they became extinct in the eleventh or twelfth century.

Bittin Furlong: the furlong part is obvious, for this is part of Mortlake South Common Field, and in this context a furlong

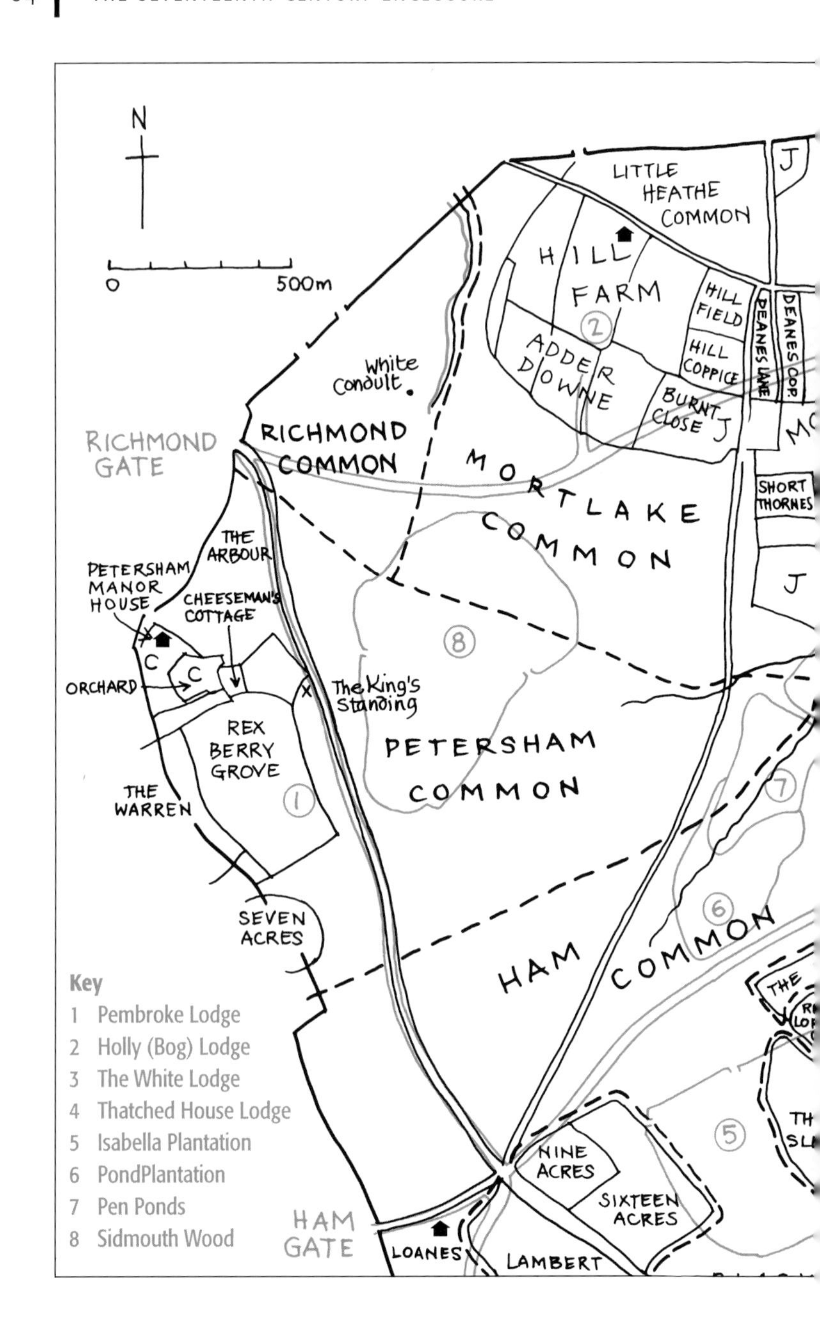
N
0
500m
LITTLE HEATHE COMMON
HILL FARM
HILL FIELD
HILL COPPICE
DEANES LANE
DEANES COP.
ADDER DOWNE
BURNT CLOSE
White Conduit
RICHMOND GATE
RICHMOND COMMON
MORTLAKE COMMON
SHORT THORNES
THE ARBOUR
PETERSHAM MANOR HOUSE
CHEESEMAN'S COTTAGE
ORCHARD
The King's Standing
REX BERRY GROVE
THE WARREN
PETERSHAM COMMON
SEVEN ACRES
HAM COMMON
NINE ACRES
SIXTEEN ACRES
HAM GATE
LOANES
LAMBERT
Key
1 Pembroke Lodge
2 Holly (Bog) Lodge
3 The White Lodge
4 Thatched House Lodge
5 Isabella Plantation
6 PondPlantation
7 Pen Ponds
8 Sidmouth Wood

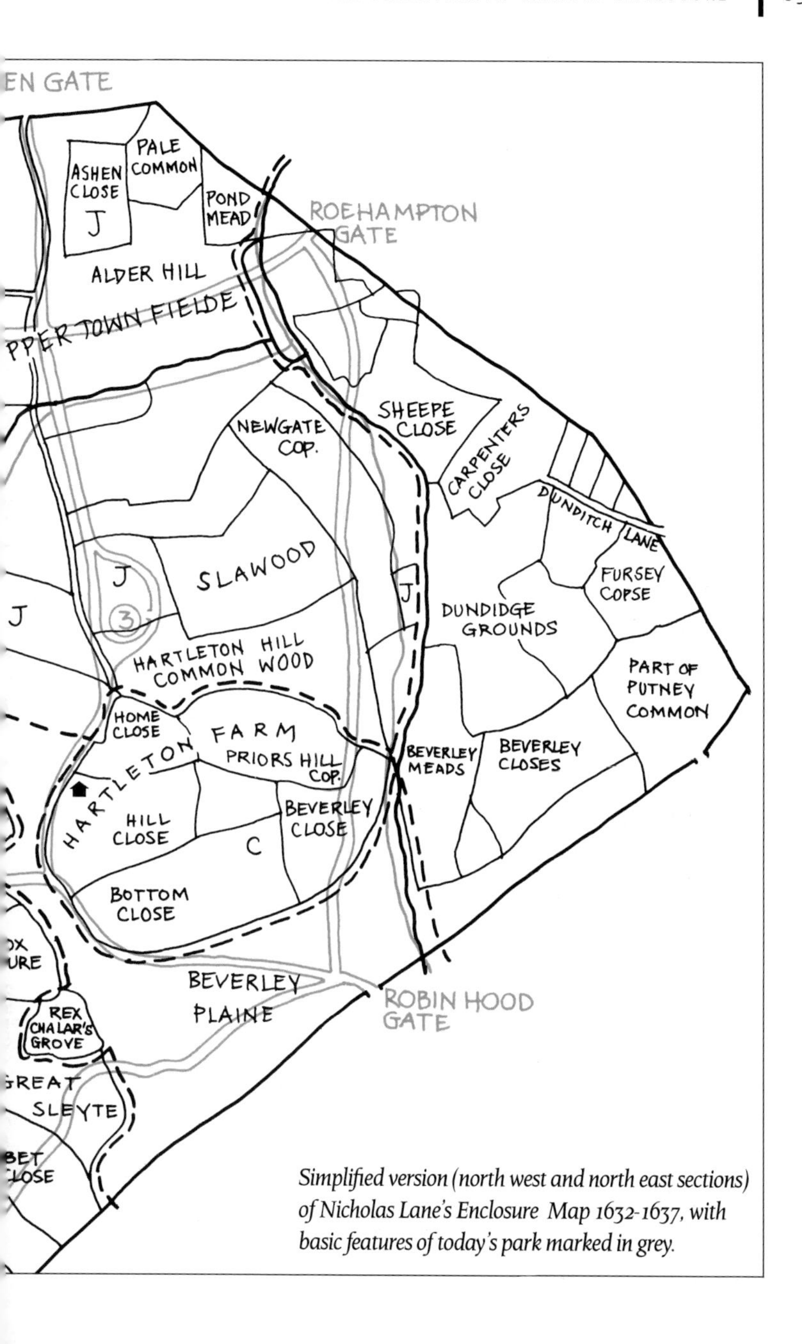

Simplified version (north west and north east sections) of Nicholas Lane's Enclosure Map 1632-1637, with basic features of today's park marked in grey.

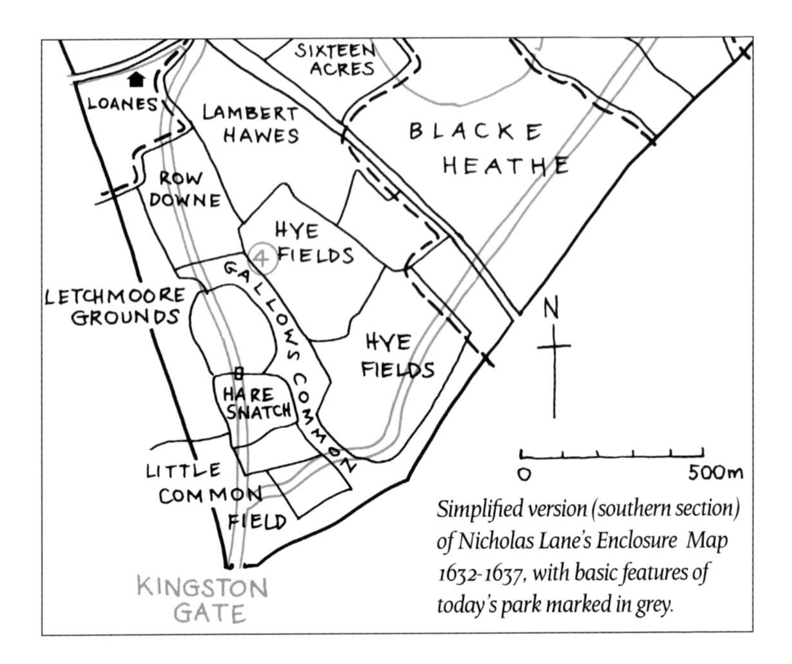

Simplified version (southern section) of Nicholas Lane's Enclosure Map 1632-1637, with basic features of today's park marked in grey.

is an arable portion of the open field, rather than a simple linear measurement. Bittin could possibly be a corruption of *bytne*, meaning the head of a valley, even though Bittin is hardly at the top of the valley, except that part belonging to Mortlake.

Chalar's Grove: if, as seems probable, this was once part of Merton Priory's holding, 'Chalar's' may be a corruption of 'chalice', indicating land funding the cost of sacramental wine, a field name that occurs elsewhere on church land.

Dundidge Grounds: this is a corruption of Dunditch, the name of a lane running from Roehampton, the end of which can be seen on Lane's map. Dun Ditch may mean 'brown ditch' but equally 'dung ditch', perhaps where night soil was dumped. One can see how the 'g' would easily be lost in pronunciation.

Fursey Close: this must indicate that gorse grew here in abundance.

Gibbet Close refers to the gibbet that stood at the roadside on top of Kingston hill. The gibbet was a metal frame in which to house the corpse of a felon hanged on the gallows further down the hill. The corpse would progressively disintegrate until a fresh one replaced it. It cannot have been a pretty sight, picked by carrion birds and with the skin progressively shrivelling off the skeleton. Siting the gibbet on top of the hill served as a permanent warning to footpads and highwaymen of the fate that awaited them if they assaulted travellers. It must have given children nightmares.

Prior's Hill Copse: this name must refer to the days of Hartington Manor, a holding of Merton Priory before the Reformation.

Slawood: this could mean a sloe or blackthorn wood, if one takes Sla- to derive from *slah*, the Anglo-Saxon for sloe, or it may be a corruption of *sloh*, meaning a mire or slough as in Slough. If one pronounces slough as in 'Slough', the apparent mis-spelling becomes clearer. A reason for plumping for this name origin is that this is a slope. A black mire does exist further to the south-west, at the foot of Prior's Hill Coppice, and there may have been a slough here also before land drains were installed.

Sleyts are sheep walks or pastures.

SOUTHERN SECTION

Black Heath: this may refer to burning. If so, the great age of the trees here suggests that the name might be very old indeed. It was probably a wood pasture, one with heath characteristics.

Gallows/Kingston Common: this refers to the gallows standing just outside what became the park.

Hare Snatch: indicates the presence of hares in what became the park. 'Snatch' may refer to a detached wood, or perhaps it might be a snare. Hares inhabited the park until c.1972. But our insistence on motorised traffic and running dogs off the leash rendered their continued presence unsustainable.

Hye fields: *hye* means 'high', the uplands overlooking Kingston.

Lambert Hawes: a *hawe* was a hedge or fence – hence 'hawthorn', the perfect hedging material. Lambert may be a proper name but more probably a corruption of 'lamb' or 'lamber', meaning a lambing place. Walk No.3 was routed through Lambert Hawes and featured (**21**) what may have been a medieval fold (see p.54).

Letchmoor or **latchmere**: a stream feeding a pond or 'mere', sometimes from which laece, or leeches, were obtained.

Loanes: probably local dialect, meaning 'lands', possibly referring to lands devoted to a particular crop but tantalisingly without further clues.

Ox Pasture and **Wheate Fields**: say what they mean.

Row Down: 'rough' down, making perfect sense on the slope running down from Thatched House Lodge into the valley.

The seventeenth century walk

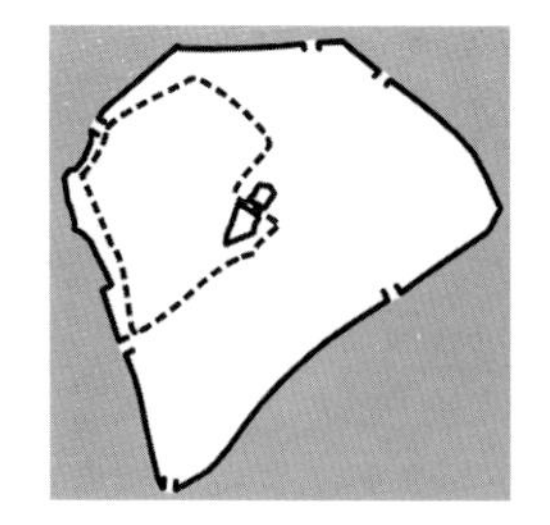

Distance 6.5km: 2 hours

Start at the Pen Ponds car park. Find the bank (23) on the map on p.00, marking the boundary of 'Rutnells'.

One of those tenanted holdings to disappear with the enclosure, clearly marked on Lane's map, was Rutnells, a separate part of Hartleton Farm. The name Rutnells remains a mystery. It was an estate with two buildings, probably a barn, a granary or a byre. With the rest of Hartleton so close, no other accommodation was likely to be required. The shape and extent of Rutnells can be imagined from Lane's map (pp.64-65), running from near the present car park down almost to the Upper Pen Pond. It can be partly followed on the ground with the help of the sketch map. As this bank approaches the car park, a veteran crab apple tree can be found, characteristically growing out of the old, possibly medieval, hedgerow bank (Tree No.1396). Crab apples grow as singletons mainly in oak woods. They were much favoured along with the hawthorn as good hedging material. A manual on good husbandry, published in 1534 states:

> 'And if thou haue pastures, thou must nedes haue quyckesettynge [hedging plants], dychynge and plasshynge. Whan it is grene, and commeth to age, then gette thy quyckesettes in the woode-countrye, and let theym be of white-thorne [hawthorn] and crabtree, for they be beste.'

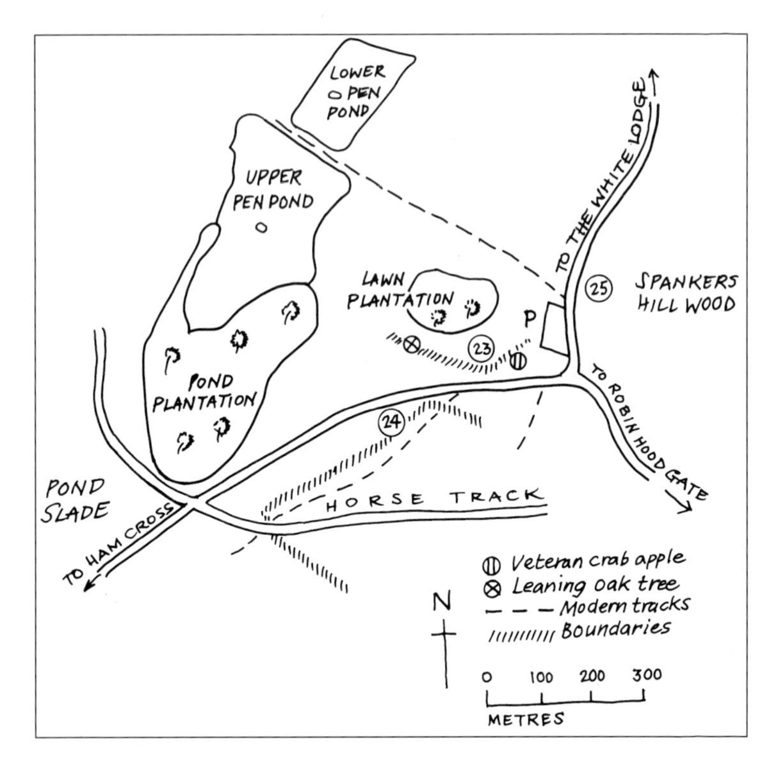

So we know how this crab apple got here, and why.

Take the road to Ham Cross, but after 200m turn half left onto a broad grassy footpath, just before two standard trees on the left of the carriageway. After 20 paces note a ditch running in at right angles from your left. This is the northern boundary of Wheate Fieldes, marked on Lane's map. Having crossed your path it turns to follow the line of the path in the form of a very slight bank on its right side. In many places this western boundary of Wheate Fieldes (24) is barely detectable, even when the summer growth has died back, but becomes clearer again as you approach the horse track (400m). Stop

immediately you have crossed the horse track to note a ditch running off at a right angle to your left.

Wheate Fieldes/Ox Pasture is clearly marked on Lane's map. You are now standing at the southwestern corner of the field. It forms part of one of the major holdings of Gregory Cole, which included The Great Sleyt, Gibbet Close and The Sleyt, thus covering an area including most of the present Isabella Plantation up to the park wall approximately from Broomfield Hill to Ladderstile Gate.

Follow the horse track (i.e turn right) back to the carriageway and walk to Ham Cross.

On your right you will pass Pond Plantation and Pond Slade (a 'slade', not to be confused with sleyt, is an open valley greensward or expanse of boggy ground), and will already have passed the Upper Pen Pond.

In 1636 Edward Manning, who was already building the park wall, was commissioned for 'railing in copses [to protect them from the deer or other livestock], the making of a pond, the cutting of lawns, etc, in the New Park at Richmond, and for bringing a river to run through the same'. Since Beverley Brook had already long been in existence, the river in question was probably that marked on Lane's map, to drain water from the slade through what became the two Pen Ponds and finally into Beverley Brook.

It is also likely that Manning's new pond was the embryo Upper Pen Pond. In 1650 we know that a punt was in use on 'the pond' and that between 1673-83 over 8,000 loads (presumably cartloads) of gravel were removed from the park for use in the local building industry. There are several gravel pits in the park, some now ponds. The Lower Pen Pond, if not the Upper, was probably the main gravel pit. Even once the Pen Ponds had been dug to their present extent, possibly at the very end of the century, they were still known as 'The Canals' indicative of the primary role to drain the slade. The original 'Pen Pond', now known as Leg of Mutton Pond, lies 200m west of the Pen Ponds. It probably acquired its name from the proximity of a deer pen. Alas, it seems to have nothing to do with the more romantic but ill-founded theory that these ponds were intentionally for 'pens', the word used for female swans in the sixteenth century.

Continue across Ham Cross, and walk 150m past the small pond in Ham Dip.

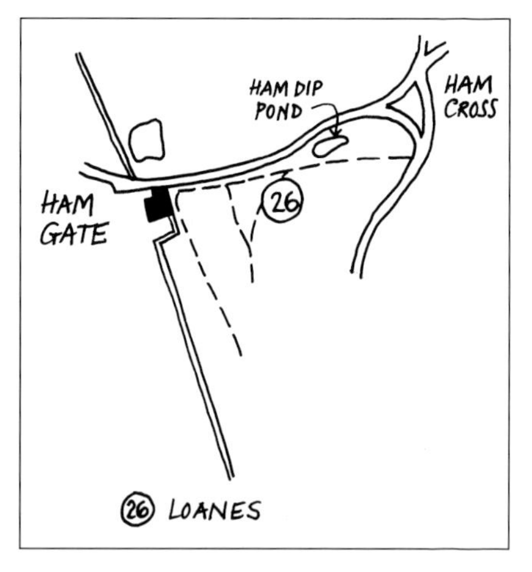

This is the site of Loanes House (**26**) in Ham that had belonged to a William Clifton. He had died in 1633 and his executor had promptly leased the buildings, three of which fell within the proposed park as shown by Lane, along with 28 acres for a period of 21 years. Now he had to negotiate the cancellation of the lease, and in 1637 surrendered this land for the park, presumably providing the new lessee with a portion of the royal compensation.

The original version of Lane's map includes a crude sketch of Loanes. The house was probably a two-storey timber framed building, infilled with brick or wattle and daub, and double gabled, possibly with two chimney stacks. These features are indicative of the major progress made in housing in the sixteenth century. A brick chimney and also either a brick or stone base that took the timber house off the wet earth had been affordable only by wealthier country people in the middle ages. Chimney technology ensured both a hotter fire and smoke free rooms, while stone or tile floors substantially reduced the level of damp. By 1600 these two features had become commonplace for virtually everyone. A century earlier all except the prosperous would still have had a central hearth, with a vent in the roof above. In fact, there had been a transformation in the standard of housing. A Spaniard who had been in England in the time of Queen Mary (1553-58), returned in the early 1600s: 'These English,' he remarked, 'had their houses of sticks and dirt, but they fare [now] commonly so well as the king.'

Indeed, there had been a craze for building in the last quarter of the sixteenth century, in the words of one contemporary:

> '... never so much hath been spent in a hundred years before as in ten year of our time; for every man almost is a builder, and he that hath bought any small parcel of ground, be it never so little, will not be quiet till he hath pulled down the old house (if any were standing) and set up a new after his own device.'

If you detect a note of disapproval, you are not mistaken. The old standards were definitely slipping:

> 'In times past, men were contented to dwell in houses builded of sallow, willow, plum tree, hardbeam [hornbeam] and elm, so that the use of oak was in manner dedicated wholly unto churches, religious houses, princes' palaces noblemen's lodgings, and navigation ...'

And what was the result?

> 'When our houses were builded of willow, then had we oaken men; but now that our houses are come to be made of oak, our men are not only become willow but a great many … altogether of straw.'

Thus by 1600 the English were really a bunch of softies. The Grumpy Old Man has always been with us.

Back to Loanes. Within a year of the enclosure all three buildings had been demolished, and the name itself transferred to the one surviving building that stood where the present Park Gate House stands, outside Ham Gate.

Turn right and walk along Ham Bottom to Petersham Gate (1.75km).

Here stood one of the principal properties inside the proposed enclosure, Petersham manor house (**27**), occupied on leasehold from Charles I's wife, Henrietta Maria, by Gregory Cole. Cole's holding was described as 'a whole tenement and a dovecote, barn, stables, etc.'. Lane depicts the main building as of contemporary design, having two chimney stacks. It had probably

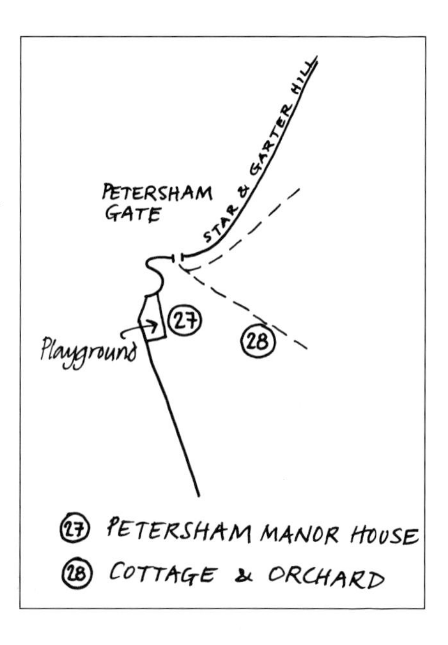

been entirely rebuilt recently or alternatively had been very substantially modernised. Two chimneys proclaimed it as the dwelling of a prosperous man.

In fact Cole held almost 800 acres in four areas of what became the park. We have already passed Rutnells and Wheate Fields (up to Ladderstile Gate) which, together with the third area on Spanker's Hill - White Lodge Hill, comprised Hartleton Farm. His Petersham holding included the adjacent lands marked Berry Grove and The Warren.

It must have been Cole of whom Clarendon wrote, 'a Gentleman, who had the best Estate, with a convenient House and Gardens, would by no means part with it'. You can understand why. Gregory had inherited the leasehold from his father, who had acquired it in 1605. He had grown up on this farmland. However, in the end he disconsolately surrendered his lands, made over his remaining leaseholds in Ham and Petersham to William Murray (soon to be Earl of Dysart and the new occupant of Ham House), and left Petersham for good. What became of him remains a mystery, but one may imagine his *schadenfreude* when King Charles began to come unstuck politically a couple of years later.

Petersham Lodge, as the manor house now became known, was not demolished (another strong indication of its fashionable appearance and appurtenances) but became accommodation for one of the first two deputy park keepers, Lodowick Carlell. Carlell was an ambitious courtier and playwright, whose father came south from Dumfriesshire on the accession of James I. He was one of the tartan mafia that flocked south to benefit from a Scottish king on the throne of England. He became master huntsman to James. Lodowick was almost the same age as Charles, and by the age of 28 or 29 held a number of court appointments. By the early 1630s he was appointed a groom of the privy chamber in the early 1630s, and also huntsman, master of the bows and keeper of the royal hounds. It sounds like a classic story of who you know, not what you know. But there is no doubting his delight as keeper in Richmond Park. In one of his plays Carlell declares:

'Most here knows
This author hunts and hawks and feeds his Deer,
Not some, but most fair days, throughout the year.'

Following his restoration in May 1660, Charles II promptly appointed new joint keepers to Richmond Park, namely the holders of the manors of Petersham and Ham, Sir Lionel Tollemache, a Suffolk gentleman and his wife, Elizabeth, Countess of Dysart and daughter of William Murray, Earl of Dysart, who as tenant had lost much manorial land to the park in 1637. Murray, like Carlell's father, was another member of the tartan mafia, who had come from Dysart in Fife. He had been appointed by James I as 'whipping boy' to Prince Charles, and in this role his own fundament had borne the chastisement rightfully due to the royal buttocks.

It is unlikely that Charles II had Murray's tingling rump in mind in making his appointment. Much more to the point, after her father's flight to France in 1645, Elizabeth had literally risked her neck as an active member of the Sealed Knot, the secret society dedicated to restoration of the Stuart monarchy. It was 'in consideration of the service done by the late Earl of Dysart and his Daughter, and of the losses sustained by then by the enclosure of the New Park' that Elizabeth and her husband received a substantial pension and the freehold of 75 acres in Petersham and Ham. But they were also awarded joint keepership of the New Park, an appointment with valuable perquisites. Although Carlell and Rogers (the second deputy keeper) were allowed to keep their households, and the immediate grazing land or 'Walks', they really had no role now and both shortly departed.

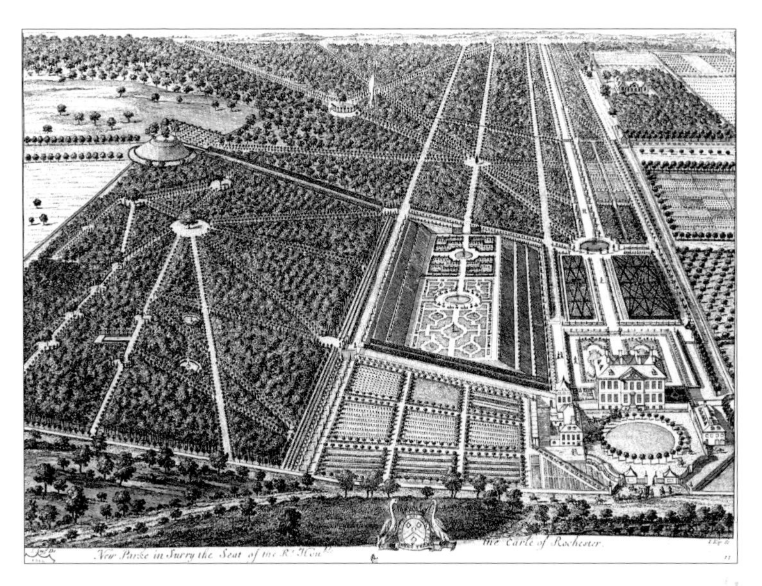

'New Park', seat of the Earl of Rochester (engraving by I. Kip, 1708 from a drawing by Leonard Knyff). Note King Henry VIII's Mound and the avenue to its left.

There had in fact been another candidate for the keepership, Sir Daniel Harvey, lord of Coombe Neville, but he stood no chance against Elizabeth who, in the words of a contemporary,

> '... was a woman of great beauty, but of far greater parts; had a wonderful quickness of apprehension, and an amazing vivacity in conversation but what ruined these accomplishments, she was restless in her ambition, profuse in her expense, and of a ravenous covetousness; nor was there anything she stuck at to compass her end, for she was violent in everything a violent friend and a much more violent enemy.'

Harvey accepted being Elizabeth's deputy keeper, but was then appointed Ambassador to the Sublime Porte, dying in Constantinople in 1672.

In the meantime, when Elizabeth was widowed in 1669 she married the Duke of Lauderdale, himself notoriously brutal. They must have made a fearsome couple, whom one would not have dared to cross. When he died in 1683, Elizabeth surrendered the Park Keepership and also Petersham Lodge, both of which passed to Lawrence Hyde, Earl of Rochester. Perhaps she had finally been outranked. Hyde, a son of Clarendon, was brother-in-law to James Duke of York (later James II) and uncle of the future Queen Anne.

In 1686 Hyde obtained a personal lease of over 50 acres in the valley, including the old Petersham Lodge which he promptly demolished and replaced with a magnificent mansion, 'New Park'. In its day New Park boasted the very latest of garden design. Samuel Molyneux, who lived in Kew and took a keen interest in gardens reported:

> '... beautiful and wildly disposed slopes.... Covered with a fine wood so intersparsed with vistas and little innumerable private dark walks.... Lin'd on both sides with low hedges.'

Indeed, each woodland glade boasted a seat, a statue, a grass plot, a basin of water or fountain. Behind the house grew at least one Cedar of Lebanon, and hornbeam walks.

It did not last very long. In 1721 a fire destroyed the house. The land was sold, and in the 1730s the Earl of Harrington commissioned Lord Burlington, the great Palladian exponent of his day, to build a new lodge. Inevitably, he also erased what he doubtless considered 'the formal mockery of princely gardens', replacing it with Arcadian parkland, an idealised natural landscape. The new 'Petersham Park' remained formally separated from the rest of Richmond Park until 1833 (see Walk No.7).

Petersham Park, front view c.1750. It was built in 1732 to a design by Lord Burlington.

Petersham Park, rear view. Note how comprehensively the landscaped park has completely erased the formal gardens of New Park in 1708. Pastoral scenes of Man in harmony with Nature replace Man in dominion over it.

Walk up the hill following the wall to Richmond Gate (1km).

A small private property, marked on Lane's map, a cottage and orchard (**28**) stood on the slopes of Petersham Park, about halfway between Petersham Gate and Pembroke Lodge. This was presumably demolished after its surrender in 1637.

From Richmond Gate follow the gravel footpath (Tamsin Trail) until there is a path across country to Conduit Wood (0.5km).

As marked on Lane's map you will find here the 'White Conduit', a brick-capped spring, more imaginatively christened 'the Bomb Shelter' by local children. The White Conduit was one of three channels cut in about 1500 to supply water to the new Palace of Shene (Richmond) on the Green. (The other two were Red Conduit, which lay on Richmond Hill probably in the area of Onslow Road, and a riverside conduit probably close to Bridge St.) The original Tudor brick part is within the south-western end of the current structure. Its name, distinguishing it from the Red Conduit, probably arose from the white mortar render or stone facing applied to the exterior brickwork. We have a good idea of what it looked like

Gallows Conduit on Coombe Hill, built by Cardinal Wolsey to supply Hampton Court Palace in c.1516. It probably resembled the White Conduit, except that it was not clad in stone or concrete render.

for two conduit houses were built in c.1516 on Coombe Hill, namely Gallows and Coombe conduits. The latter had an upper room, and its front elevation was clad in stone. It survives (on the corner of Coombe Lane and Lord Chancellor's Walk) and is still open to the public under the custodianship of English Heritage. As for the White Conduit here, we cannot be sure whether it was as large, or was of a more modest size, like Gallows Conduit. Gallows is much harder to visit, for it stands in a private garden. During repairs to the White Conduit in 1996 a Victorian brass valve was unearthed. John Cloake, with his encyclopaedic local knowledge, has speculated that this may well have been installed by Joseph Ellis, proprietor of the Star and Garter Hotel (where the Star and Garter Home now stands) from 1822 onwards. For Ellis '... found a pure spring and a perpetual one in Richmond Park and conducted the same to his own house [the Star and Garter] for general service as drinking water.' It indicates the probable route taken by the conduit to the Terrace, and thence down the hill to the palace.

Walk across to the edge of Holly (Bog) Lodge, turn left and follow perimeter around to the Riding Ring above it (0.75km).

Just on the north east side of the Riding Ring stood the two buildings of Henry White's Hill Farm (**10**), visible on Lane's map (see also Walk No.2, p.42), still just discernable by broken ground. White lived more modestly than either Clifton or Cole. Lane depicts his farmhouse with a central chimney, and with another building, presumably a barn or granary. However, his landholdings were still substantial: primarily 56 acres on Hill Farm itself, another 12 acres of arable in the Mortlake common field, 30 acres of woodland (Slawood, see its probable meaning, p.67), and also part of Beverley Close which he let to a Mr Offley.

Return to the Pen Ponds car park (2km) – the most direct route is: continue following the perimeter of Bog Lodge. When it turns right, go half right through Barn Wood, cross the carriageway and, passing Barn Wood Pond, turn up the valley running south to the Pen Ponds, cross the causeway between the two ponds and continue to the car park.

Lane shows three buildings at Hartleton. The main farmhouse (**25**) stood at the foot of Spankers Hill, close to the car park and, Lane implies, boasted two chimney stacks and a gable end. A second building apparently had one chimney.

It will be recalled that Rutnells and also the Wheate Fieldes up to Gibbet Close (separated from the rest of Hartleton by Beverley Plain) were also parts of this farm. The third section, in which the farmhouse lay, included Hill, Home, Middle and Bottom Closes, Broade Fielde, Beverley Close, and Priors Hill Copse (on Beverley Close and Priors Hill Copse, see also p.145).

Charles had allocated Hartleton Farm in 1637 to his other deputy park keeper, Humfry Rogers, someone about whom we know virtually nothing. Hartleton Farm was probably dilapidated and lacking the style and comfort of Petersham manor house. Rogers promptly rebuilt it, an indication that the farm required substantial modernisation. Courtiers and gentleman in the south-east were very particular that their houses should be in fashion. In due course it became the residence of the Keeper, after the separation of Petersham Park in 1686. In the early eighteenth century, when it acquired the name 'the Old Lodge', it was enlarged by Lord Walpole, who was Keeper at the time (see Walk No.5).

AFTERWORD

Following the execution of Charles I, Parliament vested the Corporation of the City of London in July 1649 with custodianship of the park, 'excepting timber trees'. However, with a nose for a quick profit, the Corporation immediately started felling saleable timber. Alarmed by this rampant asset-stripping, Parliament passed a Resolution the following February:

> 'That the Parliament doth declare, that it was the Intention of the Parliament in passing the Act for settling the new Park at Richmond on the Mayor and Commonalty of the City of London, that the same should be preserved as a Park still, without Destruction; and to remain as an Ornament to the City, and a Mark of Favour from the Parliament unto the said City.'

In 1660 the Corporation moved swiftly to mend its fences with the restored monarchy. It handed the park over to Charles II within four days of his Restoration.

Some sixty years later George I urgently needed £2,000 and proposed selling park timber. His Surveyor-General, possibly mindful of Parliament's previous ruling, sternly reminded him 'the wood in Richmond Park is rather for ornament than profit.'

The Park in the eighteenth century

In 1727 George II appointed Robert, Lord Walpole, as Ranger, though it was his father, Sir Robert Walpole, the Prime Minister, who exercised effective superintendence and enjoyed the benefit. Sir Robert was already a passionate hunter in the park and for the next quarter century the park was regularly used for this purpose. Another avid hunter was that most zestful of women, Lady Mary Wortley Montagu, best known for her letters from Turkey, who at the age of 35 wrote to her sister:

> 'I pass many hours on horseback, and I'll assure you, ride stag hunting, which I know you'll stare to hear of. I have arrived to vast courage and skill that way, and am so well pleased with it as with the acquisition of a new sense. His Royal Highness [later George II] hunts in Richmond Park, and I make one of the beau monde of his train. I desire you after this account not to name the word old woman to me any more. I approach to fifteen nearer than I did ten years ago, and am in hopes to improve every year in health and vivacity.'

Sir Robert Walpole himself was so devoted to the chase that he retired to the Old Lodge (old Hartleton Farm), which he had extensively remodelled, for Saturdays as well as Sundays, instructing the Commons to abandon its previous habit of sitting on Saturdays. It is thus that we arguably owe the two-day week-end to hunting in Richmond Park. Indeed, in one portrait he stands in the park with his hounds around him, the Old Lodge in the background. Sir Robert died in 1745, his son six years later in 1751. In the early nineteenth century the Old Lodge fell into disrepair and was demolished in 1841.

There was wild turkey shooting too. Turkey had been introduced to Britain in 1521, and into the Richmond Park in about 1690. In the early eighteenth century there were probably over 3,000 turkeys in the park. Dogs were used to flush them from the extensive gorse up into the trees where they could be shot.

If pollarding of the oaks continued into the eighteenth century it may partly have been in order to ensure that these wild turkeys settled in lower branches where they could more easily be bagged. Edward Jesse, writing in 1834, has this to say:

> 'One of the keepers in Richmond Park informs me that he has often heard his father, who was also a keeper, mention that, in the reign of George the second, a large flock of wild turkies, consisting of not less than three thousand, was regularly kept up as part of the stock of the park. They were hunted with dogs, and made to take refuge in a tree where they were frequently shot by George the second. I have not been able to learn how long they had been preserved in the park before his reign, but they were totally destroyed towards the latter end of it, in consequence of the dangers to which the keepers were exposed in protecting them from poachers, with whom they had many bloody fights, being frequently overpowered by them.'

The park more or less ceased to be a deer-hunting park after the Walpoles' demise and became more of a farm to provide venison for the royal and ministerial households. By the end of the century sport consisted of hare coursing, angling and partridge and pheasant shooting.

Management of the park and its deer required the provision of housing for the various keepers and a number of houses appeared. These form the basis of Walk No.5.

A PLAN
of his Majesty's
NEW PARK,
at Richmond in Surrey.
Taken Sep: 1754.
By Edwd. John Eyre. Surveyor.
Richmond Hill
Gate
The Earl of Harrington's
The Dutchess of Argyle's
Mole Catchers
White Ash Lodge
Bearing to Ham
HAM
COMMON
Ham Gate
Kingston
Corner Gate
Gallows Hill
now a Bridle Gate
a Bridle

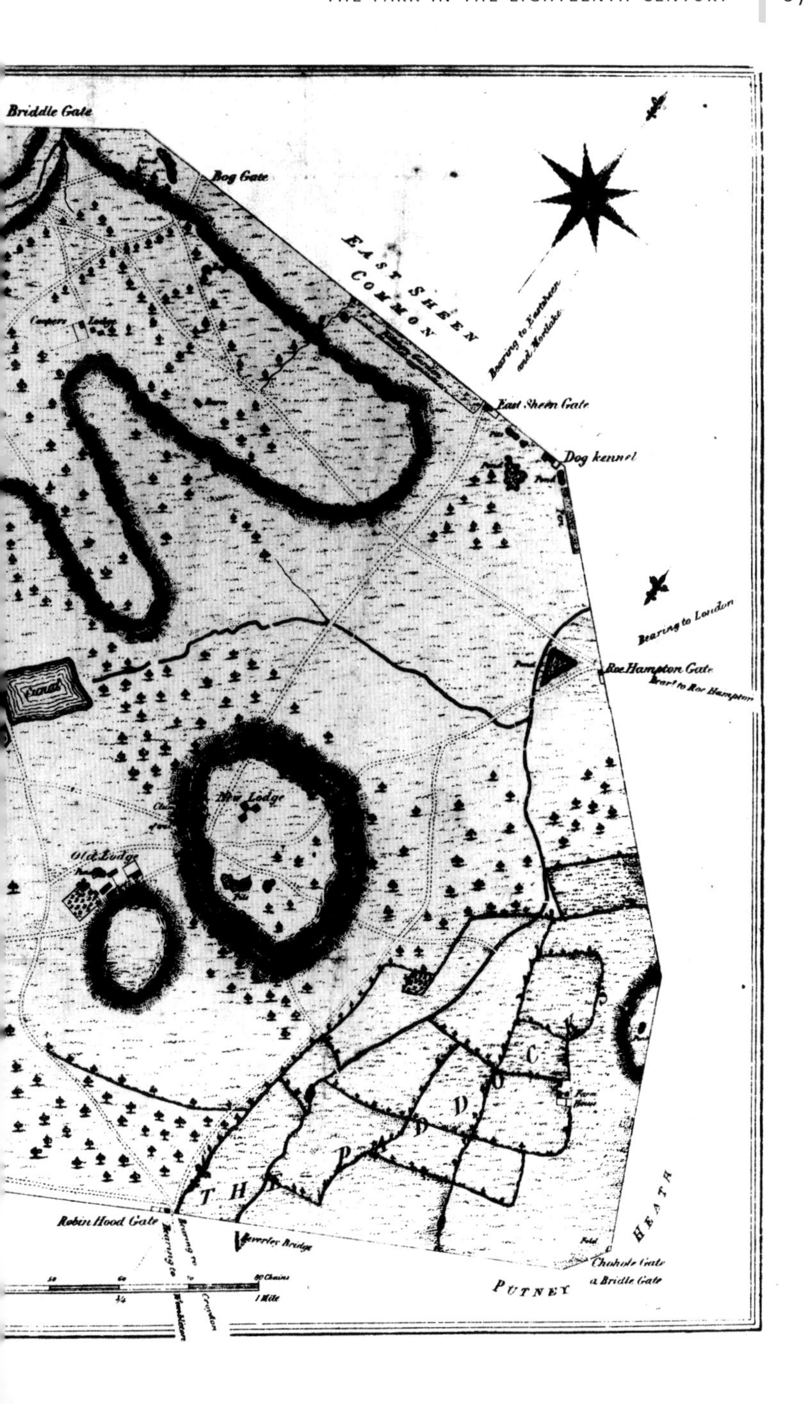
Briddle Gate
Bog Gate
EAST SHEEN COMMON
Bearing to Eastsheen and Mortlake
East Sheen Gate
Dog kennel
Bearing to London
Roe Hampton Gate
Bear^t to Roe Hampton
Old Lodge
Robin Hood Gate
Beverley Bridge
Chohole Gate a Bridle Gate
PUTNEY HEATH
Farm House
80 Chains
1 Mile

WALK 5

The eighteenth century buildings walk

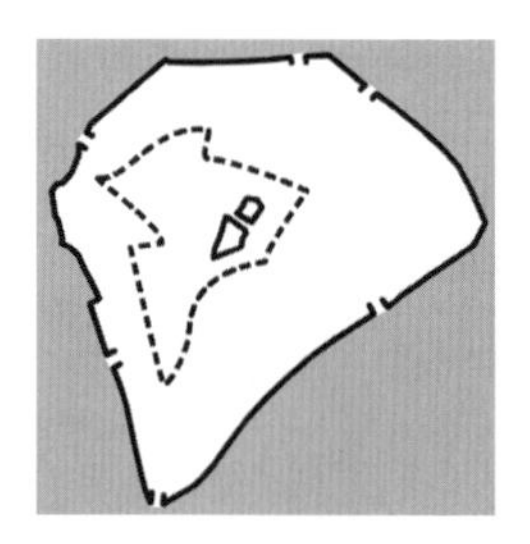

Distance 8km: 2 hours

Start: Pembroke Lodge car park. Enter Pembroke Lodge gardens front entrance.

Pembroke Lodge has humble origins. It was originally the Molecatcher's cottage but during George II's reign was known as Hill Lodge and occupied by one of the park gamekeepers. It must have been enlarged at this time. It stood among the oak trees of Berry Grove, the pre-enclosure wood that grew on the escarpment and slope here.

It was probably in the late 1780s that Eliza, Countess of Pembroke, persuaded George III to lease her the property. She had become a lady of the bedchamber in 1782, a position she retained until Queen Charlotte's death in 1818. It proved a tricky appointment since, during his periods of madness, George III imagined himself married to her. His infatuation went back to the days of their youth, when she had been a court beauty with 'the face of a Madonna', as Horace Walpole had put it. She was now over 50 and the king's attentions rendered her situation with the Queen embarrassing. She was pursued, according to one witness, 'with so much ardour and such splendid offers that I tremble for her virtue'. It must have been an ordeal, particularly in view of her own unhappy marriage. Eliza, however, remained above reproach and following his recovery wrote to the king with touching grace:

> 'Your Majesty has always acted by me as the kindest brother as well as the most gracious of sovereigns... if I might presume to say that I felt like the most affectionate sister towards an indulgent brother, it would exactly express my sentiments.'

As for the king, he reproached the Earl of Pembroke for treating his wife so badly. Pembroke retorted with a brutally lewd comment on his spouse. So much for *noblesse oblige*.

Back to the building. Sir John Soane remodelled and enlarged the property for her in the period 1785-95, but it was impossible to disguise its mongrel, hotchpotch origins. By the time of her death in 1831, at the ripe old age of 94, Pembroke Lodge had acquired its present form and her name.

Pembroke Lodge was granted to Lord John Russell in 1847, one year after he had become Prime Minister. It remained in the Russell household until 1929. (For the Russells, see Walk No.7 and for the Russell School, see Walk No.9.)

The veteran oak trees in the surrounding gardens are the remnant of Berry Grove (see map on p.64).

Retrace your steps, cross the carriageway and proceed around the northern side of Sidmouth Wood, crossing the Richmond-Roehampton carriageway, to Holly (Bog) Lodge (1 km).

In spite of the extra buildings, the lodge, probably constructed in the mid-1730s, retains great charm. It seems always to have been the head keeper's lodge. It may be the enlargement of a building originally known as Cooper's Lodge, presumably lived in by Joseph Cooper and his son Augustine (buried in Petersham churchyard, 1735 and 1775 respectively). The Coopers may well have been head keepers in their day, but we do not know for sure.

Holly (Bog) Lodge in the eighteenth century.

In 1771 it became known as Lucas' Lodge, and one may infer that this was when Augustine Cooper retired and John Lucas assumed the office of head keeper.

Lucas was almost certainly the son of a Lucas recruited from the Duke of Newcastle's estate at Claremont (Esher) at the beginning of the century, a man renowned for his prowess in tackling poachers with the quarterstaff. John Lucas died in 1795 and, since his own son, John, was deemed too young, he was succeeded by his deputy, James Sawyer, who had joined the park staff only eight years earlier but whose family had been engaged in deer-keeping for generations. Thus, James Sawyer moved into the head keeper's lodge and the young John Lucas moved out to the deputy keeper's house, White Ash Lodge (see below). It was very briefly known as Holly Lodge at the beginning of the twentieth century, but had previously acquired the name of Bog Lodge, on account of the bog to its north, drained only in the mid-nineteenth century. 'Bog' was considered inappropriate for visiting schoolchildren and it was renamed Holly Lodge in the 1990s, but with the loss of its name we lose a clue to the landscape.

Walk back along the access road to Holly Lodge, cross the main carriageway and walk 200m beyond, until the Queen's Ride lies on your left.

The Queen's Ride was probably cut through existing open woodland. It was essential to the vista from the White Lodge but it was also the final part of the private road completed for Queen Caroline, George II's consort, who habitually travelled between Richmond Lodge in the Old Deer Park and this new hunting lodge that soon became her favourite residence. She entered the park from Kew at Queen's Gate (now Bog Gate), which had been specially cut through the wall for her.

Walk the Queen's Ride to the White Lodge (1.2km).

The White Lodge, first known as Stone Lodge (on account of its Portland stone facing) and then as New Lodge to differentiate it from Old (Hartleton) Lodge 500 metres away (discussed in Walk No.4), was built in the Palladian style in 1727. It was designed by Roger Morris in partnership with his patron, the Earl of Pembroke. They had already built Marble Hill, much more of an architectural landmark, a couple of years previously.

One might question the siting of the two great houses so close together but they commanded about the best views in the park. Proximity may also have reflected the intimate relations between the royal family and the prime minister. George I, who did not live to see the lodge completed, greatly enjoyed Walpole's company hunting. After his death Queen Caroline and Sir Robert Walpole became close political allies, 'the two ears' of George II. Princess Amelia lived here when appointed ranger, 1751-61 (see Walk No.6).

The White Lodge was originally designed like Marble Hill with a hipped roof, shaped like a pyramid. It seems that this was abandoned in favour of a shallow mansard, as in this early illustration.

When George III took over the rangership in 1792 he immediately took an interest in the park, initiating extensive but unsuccessful attempts to drain boggy areas. He re-routed the Richmond - Roehampton carriageway away from the north side to Holly (Bog) Lodge to its present route, to maximise the aesthetic pleasure from the landscape of the park (as any car driver should notice). He also experimented with new agricultural methods on what is now the golf course. Sickness forced his retirement as Ranger in 1814.

Sadly, the White Lodge quickly lost its architectural integrity as a hunting box. Princess Amelia commissioned the construction of two side pavilions. These were designed by Stephen Wright, erstwhile clerk to the great landscape architect, William Kent, and they resemble the side pavilions of Horse Guards, one of Kent's better known works. These slightly compromised the original effect, but the single storey colonnades to the side pavilions minimised the visual impact of these extensions.

George III had used the White Lodge but never lived in it. In 1801 he insisted that his newly appointed prime minister, Henry Addington, should live at the White Lodge. Addington had a hard time as prime minister, deliberately undermined by Pitt and others. He unfairly became an object of ridicule. In 1803 Canning, a political opponent, coined a damaging couplet which amused even street urchins:

'Pitt is to Addington
As London is to Paddington.'

It is not easy to come back from such an unforgettable put-down. It helped to leave Addington politically emasculated. He resigned in 1804 but was able to stay on at the White Lodge. The following year he was ennobled as Viscount Sidmouth. In 1813 he took over the management of the park as deputy-ranger (see Walk No.7), something he was very much more successful at.

George III was anxious that the White Lodge, still really only a hunting pavilion, should be large enough for Addington and his family, and he commissioned James Wyatt, the Gothic revivalist, to convert the property into a country house. Wyatt already had a controversial reputation. His restorations of medieval cathedrals had already earned him the epithet 'The Destroyer'. Now he was given a free hand and he duly spoilt the appearance of the White Lodge with two-storey corridors leading to modified flank pavilions.

Meanwhile, the first man actually to describe himself as a landscape gardener, Humphry Repton (1752-1818), was set to work on the grounds in 1805. He had been a student of Lancelot 'Capability' Brown. Repton always prepared a 'Red Book',

Humphry Repton's landscape proposals: before.

his manuscript proposals bound in red morocco. Like other contemporaries, Repton usually favoured a vista of raw nature after the more contrived landscapes of the mid-eighteenth century. But the White Lodge was a good deal more public than a private park. He considered, but abandoned, ideas of a ha-ha (a ditch concealing a fence, a gardening feature introduced to Britain in the early years of the century), which he considered would leave the garden too public, and alternatively of a belt of trees and shrubs, which he decided would prove too enclosed. Then, he uncharacteristically opted for what he called 'the ancient formal style', commending 'the neatness and security of a gravel walk' to replace the 'uncleanly, pathless grass of a forest, filled with troublesome animals of every kind, and some occasionally dangerous'. His Red Book 'before' illustration, suggests the mayhem caused by deer and other livestock, not to mention casually abandoned hurdles, convincing evidence of

Humphry Repton's landscape proposals: after.

how plucky we are to stroll in such deer-infested pastures. Today the White Lodge stands at the centre of a complex of buildings. While Repton's formal garden has disappeared, Wyatt's additions remain. Fortunately, the key view from the Queen's Ride, for many years marred by the feather-edged wooden fence, will be reopened to recover its appearance.

Walk along the tarmac carriageway to the Pen Ponds car park.

The Old Lodge at the foot of Spanker's Hill remained the regular home of the Deputy Ranger until the early nineteenth century when it became little used, and then fell into disrepair and was finally demolished in 1841. What is remarkable is that virtually no surface traces remain, except for a circular depression probably marking the site of a well, up the slope just behind the house, and also a few bricks lying in the ground.

The Old Lodge, by Francis Grose, c.1760. Note the punt on the Upper Pen Pond.

Take the carriageway to Ham Cross, but strike half left after 100m along a broad grassy path. Follow it, across the horse track, until you reach the Disabled car park on the edge of the Isabella Plantation. Continue straight across, crossing another horse track down into the gully, crossing the brick culvert, and up the far side to Thatched House Lodge (2.5km).

Thatched House Lodge probably originated as a small building constructed for deer keepers in the 1670s. It seems to have been inhabited by a Charles Aldridge, buried in Petersham churchyard in 1736. It was about this time that Sir Robert Walpole provided money for the improvement of Aldridge's Lodge. Sixty years later the frontage was apparently remodelled by Soane, no doubt on the basis of his work on Pembroke Lodge and the Richmond Gate.

The building first appears as 'Thatched House Lodge' in a map of 1771, probably on account of the thatched summer house in the garden, which Walpole had constructed in 1727 to entertain fellow hunters, including the king, at the end of the chase. In the 1780s

The Old Lodge, c.1780. It looks as if the outbuildings have been cleared away in favour of an ornamental pond..

the interior of the Thatched House (composed of two octagonal rooms) was decorated, probably by the Venetian Antonio Zucchi (1726-95), husband of Angelica Kauffmann. Zucchi was Robert Adam's chief decorative painter. The paintings were removed for safekeeping in the 1960s. You may obtain a restricted view of the Thatched House by walking around the north side of the Lodge grounds.

Walk northwards, back towards Pembroke Lodge. Turn off to the right, down the carriageway to White Ash Lodge (1.5km).

White Ash Lodge was probably built at about the same time as Bog Lodge, in the 1730s or 1740s to accommodate the deputy keeper. It retains its charm, though the adjacent stable is in an advanced state of neglect. It will be recalled that James Sawyer had moved to Bog Lodge on his accession as head keeper in 1795.

When he died in 1825 John Lucas, who had been too young to assume headship in 1795, was now invited to take up the post denied him then. Lucas apparently declined in favour of Sawyer's own son since he would have been obliged to move to Bog Lodge. He could not bear the thought of turning James Sawyer's widow and family out of the home they had enjoyed for 30 years. Apparently the two families lived intimately, frequently dining together. Both families were employed in the park for well over a century.

Return to Pembroke Lodge car park (1 km).

Three other eighteenth century buildings, Ladderstile Cottage, Ham Gate Lodge and Bishop's Lodge are mentioned in Walk No.6.

The eighteenth century right of access (perimeter) walk

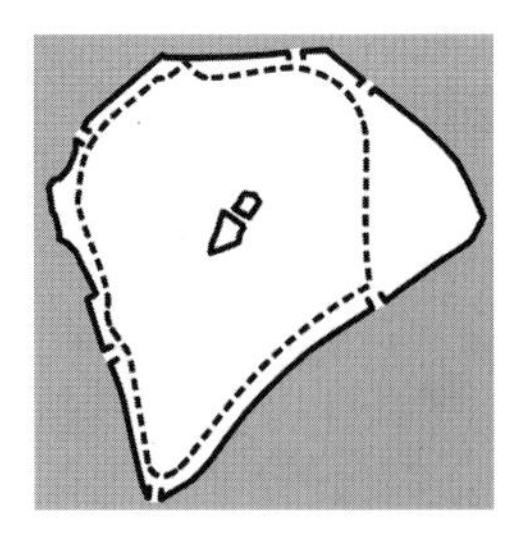

Distance 14km: 3 hours

This walk tells the story of how the fight for public access was won and gives a brief outline of points of interest around the perimeter, including the origins of each gate.

In order to give a chronological account of the struggle for public access, this walk starts at Cambrian Gate. (However you may start from any gate you choose if you simply wish to walk the park perimeter, reading the relevant notes for each gate.) Turn left and make your way along path bordering the park wall for 400m down to the gully where the stream flows under the park wall. You may care to find a log to sit on while reading the following.

First, a minor diversion: note the magnificent poplar standing by the stream, close to the wall (Tree No.1075). It is a Native Black Poplar, of which only about 3,000 recorded specimens still survive in England, half of which grow in the Vale of Aylesbury. It looks somewhat like the hybrid black and grey poplars, but its bark tends to have more burrs. It has another characteristic: in maturity the very ends of its shoots tend to curve upwards, almost vertically. Its crucial distinguishing mark, however, on which there can be little chance of error, is the gall created by an aphid on the stalk of its leaf. Only the Lombardy poplar, easily distinguishable by its shape, shares this distinction. It is, in the words of the countryside historian, Oliver Rackham, 'the last shadow of the vanished flood plain wildwood'. So, this magnificent tree (and its truncated neighbour) is a rarity we should treasure. The Royal Parks have a small propagation programme for this rare tree.

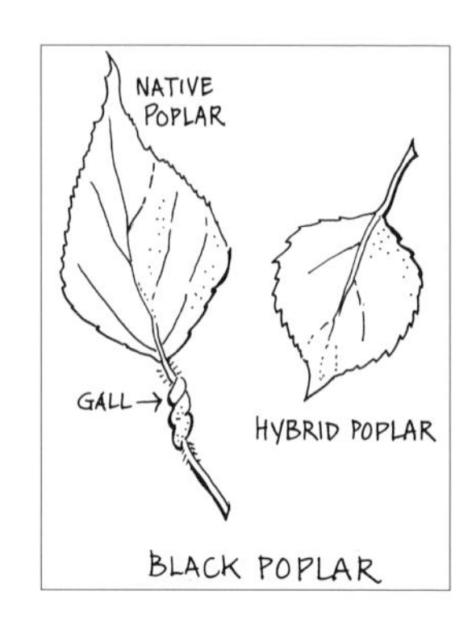

Our right to walk in Richmond Park is in good measure thanks to a local man in the middle of the eighteenth century. Charles I had built a two-metre high wall to enclose the park but allowed complete freedom both to the public to cross the new park from one village or town to another and for the poor to gather firewood. These liberalities were, no doubt, to avoid offending local people who had traditionally used the common pasture and woodland.

Six gates were put in the 1637 wall of enclosure, where the present Richmond, East Sheen, Roehampton, Robin Hood, Ladderstile and Ham Gates are located. Almost exactly a century later access became progressively restricted and then virtually impossible in the 1750s. The present wall is largely eighteenth century, though it has been patched and repaired in many places since then.

The park had been enclosed to provide hunting for the king and his cronies. It was, perhaps, inevitable that local people with free access came to watch the royals at play, hunting stags and shooting wild turkey (with which the park was so liberally supplied, see Walk No.5). In 1673 park gates had already been locked to prevent unauthorized farm livestock from grazing in the

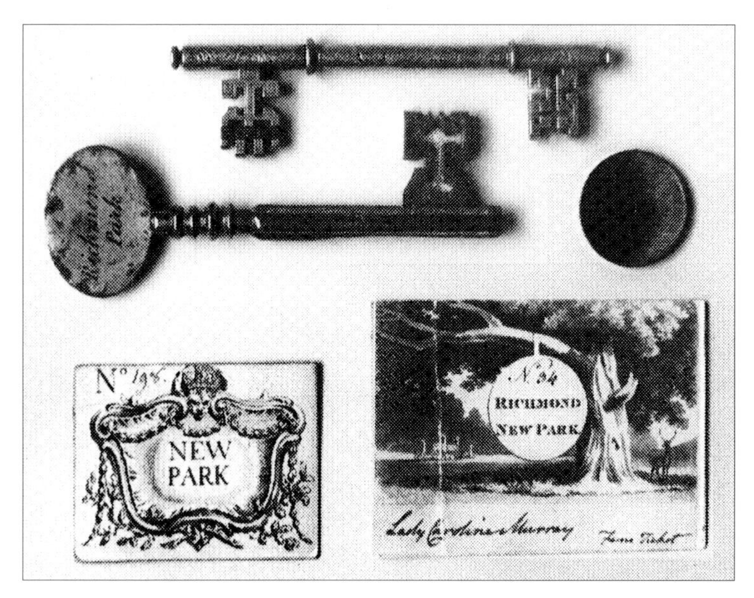

Keys and admission tickets to Richmond Park.

park. Ladderstiles were installed to allow people continued free access. By the mid1730s so many people came to spectate that they were considered 'not only troublesome but very dangerous'. In 1735 George II's consort, Queen Caroline, authorised the issue of a notice to the effect that admittance in future would be allowed only to those with a 'hunting ticket' obtainable from the ranger. It was the carriage and mounted spectators who were the main problem, and many of these had acquired their own keys to the gates. The locks were now changed, and some of the ladderstiles removed. In 1742 Walpole built lodges at the gates to admit 'all respectable persons' during daylight, but the restrictions were already creating considerable resentment in the locality.

In April 1751 Princess Amelia, George II's youngest daughter, succeeded Lord Walpole as Ranger. Amelia was unusual, described by a contemporary as 'a masculine woman, fond of

Beating the bounds of Richmond Parish, May 1751.

being in the stables, and an inveterate snufftaker'. In spite of or because of these qualities, she was her father's favourite daughter, but to the people surrounding the park she was a minx, for she resolved to make it wholly private.

Barely six weeks after her appointment, a Richmond Parish party, led by the vicar, made its annual Ascension Day ritual of beating the bounds of the parish, which included a slice of the park (see Nicholas Lane's map, page 64). When the party members had beaten the bounds as far as the park wall, precisely where the stream exits, they found to their dismay that not only was the bridle gate on the parish boundary locked as was normal, but that the usual ladderstile was missing. Furthermore their progress was under observation by three men sitting on the wall. Whether the vicar, churchwarden and others actually broke part of the wall or climbed over a delapidated section, as a contemporary illustration suggests, they successfully entered the park, still closely observed by the same trio, now on horseback. Having beaten the bounds within the park, the party left by

Richmond Gate, barely 50 metres from the point at which the parish boundary crosses the park wall on Star and Garter Hill.

It seems to have been the pretext Princess Amelia sought. For she now closed the park to all foot, horse and carriage traffic, only allowing her personal guests entry. Horace Walpole at Strawberry Hill watched with interest, particularly since his brother had preceded her as Park Ranger and his father had regularly hunted there:

> 'She preserved no measures of popularity... Petitions were presented to her, but she would not receive them; they were printed in the public newspapers but had as little effect.'

If there was any comfort at all for the local citizenry, it must have been that the nobility, too, was given short shrift, as Walpole wryly observed:

> 'Lord Brooke, who has taken the late Duchess of Rutland's [house] at Petersham, asked for a key. The answer was (mind it, for it was tolerably mortifying for an Earl) "that the Princess had already refused one to my Lord Chancellor."'

Every effort was made to shame the Princess into moderating her position. It was the mainly carriage-using gentry that brought the first court action against her, or rather against one of her gatekeepers at Croydon Assizes in 1754, but they lost their case. Significantly, one of the presiding judges, Mr Justice Foster, hinted that they had lost their case because they had failed to distinguish between a footway, a highway and a cartway. (The story continues at East Sheen Gate).

Proceed along the park wall towards East Sheen Gate, pausing at Bog Gate.

Bog Gate (or Queen's Gate): In 1736 the owners of Sheen Common issued a licence permitting Queen Caroline, George II's wife, to make a road to the 'new gate in the wall of the park' which had just been pierced for her. She used it as her private entrance for her journeys between Richmond Lodge (a royal residence in the Old Deer Park) and the White Lodge in the park. It became known as Bog Gate on account of a marshy area south east of the gate eventually drained in 1855. The Inns of Court Rifle Volunteers were permitted to use the gate in 1870 on their way to drill on the ground between the gate and Holly (Bog) Lodge. Membership was popular among young men at this time. Public access was granted 24 hours a day in 1894 and the present 'cradle' gate installed, probably the first for the park. From 1906 the metal-fenced enclosure on the west side of Bog Gate was used as the Richmond Rifle Club's range.

Proceed past Teck Plantation.

Kitchen Garden Gate, hidden behind Teck Plantation, is located at the western end of the Ranger's Garden. It is probably a nineteenth century gate and has never been used by the public. Teck Plantation commemorates the residence of the Duke and Duchess of Teck at the White Lodge. Their daughter became George v's consort, Queen Mary.

Proceed to East Sheen Gate.

Note on the left, set into the fencing of the present gate lodge, one of the old 'shelter boxes'. These were used by the 'Park Keeping Force', precursors of the Royal Parks Constabulary particularly in inclement weather. Another such lodge may be found towards the northern end of Pembroke Lodge Grounds, equipped with a fireplace and bookshelves. Nice to know they produced vulnerable as well as super humans in the age of empire, and on a wet day what could be better than settling in front of a roaring fire with a good book? A police force was first established in 1854, after a guest of the Russells walking through the park was relieved of her watch and jewellery at pistol point. (Shelter boxes also once existed by the barrow ((**3**) on Walk No.1) above Ham Gate, and on the southern side of Spanker's Hill.

East Sheen Gate: (*You may wish to take a seat by Adam's Pond to read this.*) For anyone who values free use of the park this gate must be visited. For it was here in 1755 that John Lewis, a Richmond brewer, asserted the pedestrian right of entry, to use a *footway*, after Princess Amelia had denied it. An admirer of John Lewis, Gilbert Wakefield, recorded what happened:

> 'Lewis takes a friend with him to the spot, waits for the opportunity of a carriage passing through, and when the gatekeeper was shutting the gate, interposed and offered to go in. "Where is your ticket?" "What occasion for a ticket – anybody may pass through here?" "No, not without a ticket." "Yes, they may." "No, not without a ticket." "Yes, they may, and I will." "You shan't." "I will." The woman pushed; Lewis suffered the door to be shut upon him…'

John Lewis, by Thomas Stewart.

Armed with the evidence of an eyewitness, John

Lewis took his case against the gatekeeper, Martha Gray, to the Kingston Assize. It took three years to get his case heard, but after a day's trial on 3 April 1758, the verdict went against the unfortunate 'jobsworth' Martha Gray. The presiding judge was none other than Michael Foster, who had ruled against carriage rights four years earlier. Foster was nobody's pushover. He was a Protestant dissenter who had resisted pressure to become an Anglican, the expected identity for anyone called to the bar. One future Lord Chancellor, on reading the verdict, expressed

> 'great pleasure ... that we have one English judge, whom nothing can tempt or frighten, ready and able to hold up the laws of his country as a great shield of the rights of the people.'

Beyond what one might describe as the petty issues of the parish pump, therefore, one may take this case as an early one in the progressive triumph of the law over the vested interests of the powerful in the land in the second half of the eighteenth century.

Wakefield continues Lewis' story:

> 'After the decree in his favour, Lewis was asked, whether he would have a step ladder to go over the wall, or a door? He hesitated for some minutes; but reflecting that strangers might not be aware of the privilege of admission through a door, which could not stand open on account of the deer; considering also that in process of time a bolt might be put on this door, and then a lock, and so his efforts be gradually frustrated; sensible too that a step ladder, at the first inspection, would signify its use to every beholder, he preferred that mode of introduction.'

On 12 May 1758 ladder-stiles were fixed to East Sheen and Ham Gates, and on 16th May were thrown open, when 'a vast concourse of people from all the neighbouring villages climbed over the ladder stiles into the park.'

It was not quite the end of the story. John Lewis had to return to court, for Princess Amelia tried to thwart its will by designing ladders with the rungs spaced so far apart that the very young and the old could not negotiate them. She was tersely instructed by the court to provide ladders that were easy to climb.

Such was John Lewis' celebrity that his portrait was painted by Thomas Stewart, a pupil of Sir Joshua Reynolds. (Reynolds, incidentally, lived at Wick House on Richmond Hill's Terrace.) The painting now hangs in Richmond Reference Library, and an engraving made with the following inscription by Gilbert's brother, Thomas Wakefield, the vicar of St Mary Magdalene, the parish church of Richmond:

> 'Be it remembered That by the steady Perseverance of John Lewis, Brewer, at Richmond Surry, the Right of a Free Passage through Richmond Park was recovered after being upwards of twenty Years withheld from the People.'

Shortly afterwards Lewis's brewery, not far from the Terrace Gardens, was inundated by a major flood. He was ruined, living in poverty till his death in 1792, aged 80, supported by an annual subscription by inhabitants of Richmond. It was, predictably, Thomas Wakefield, who had organised this small pension, as a debt of gratitude to a courageous man.

Nor would you wish to remain in ignorance of Gilbert Wakefield, our storyteller. He knew a thing or two about being the wrong side of authority, though like Foster and Lewis, he was impressed neither by the mighty nor by the conventions of the age. Wakefield was a man without wealth but with integrity in spades. A theologian who had entered the Anglican priesthood, he concluded that he could assent neither to the Trinity nor the Incarnation and so, without regard to his own material well-being, renounced his living with the prospect of a future life of straitened means. Having renounced Anglicanism, he also took on the government. In 1798 William Pitt declared war on France. Wakefield wrote a powerful anti-war pamphlet and was promptly charged with seditious libel. He chose to defend himself, in the words of one admirer, 'his simplicity quite apostolic, his courage purely heroic'. But he did not have a Foster for his judge. He was fined £500 and sent to Dorchester gaol for two years. Almost overnight his friends raised £5,000 for the support of his family. The great radicals of the day flocked to Dorchester to applaud him. Never wealthy, Wakefield said he owed his fortune entirely to His Majesty's attorney-general.

Carriage owners were now emboldened to bring their own case in 1760 for use of the carriage and bridleways, but they were again unsuccessful. By now, however, Princess Amelia's local standing could hardly have been worse and she resigned the Rangership the following year. On assuming the office of Ranger himself in 1792, George III relaxed the prohibition on carriages. Given today's problem with cars, you would have good grounds for believing that this was a catastrophic error of judgement. The present double gates date from 1926.

We like to think of John Lewis as our local hero. Yet he also surely stands alongside Wakefield and Foster in the pantheon of British Worthies of this heroic age.

Proceed towards Roehampton Gate.

Patches and irregularities in the wall 200m from East Sheen Gate mark the remains of Sheen Cottage (see Walk No.9).

About 100 metres east of these traces of Sheen Cottage another mature native black poplar may be found (Tree No.1094), close to the wall just after an angle in the latter.

Approaching Roehampton Gate note the major surface drainage ditches running to the park wall. The original ditches were probably part of George III's endeavours at the end of the eighteenth century.

Roehampton Gate: One of the six original gates. For part of the nineteenth century and probably previously, the park authorities had to pay a quit rent of one buck a year for the right of way, as the gate opened upon private property. The present wrought iron carriage gates date from 1899.

Follow the path beside Beverley Brook to Robin Hood Gate, since the land north of Beverley Brook, including Chohole Gate is inaccessible except to golfers.

Beverley Brook rises at Worcester Park and enters the Thames at Barn Elms Park, Putney. The brook sustained brown trout in the eighteenth century. But it was treated brutally in the twentieth century, many of its meanderings straightened out and canalised in the interests of efficient outflow, but contrary to the interests of the natural world. It was adopted as the outflow of Worcester Park Sewage works, thus killing off the fish. In the 1930s concrete walls were built in places, making it impossible for the few water voles which inhabited the stream here. Since then the concrete has been removed, and in the late 1990s the sewage outflow removed, rendering the water clean. By 2005 five or six different fish species had returned, among them sticklebacks, which has drawn the first kingfishers back. It is too expensive to re-cut the original path of the brook, but it is intended to create flood and wet areas, and ensure suitable habitats for water voles on the feeder streams on the golf course. In short, a serious attempt to encourage the natural profusion of previous centuries.

[**Chohole Gate**: Lies in the extreme south-east corner of the park. It is first mentioned in 1680 when a warrant was issued 'to cause the grass now growing in the paddock near Chohole Gate to be cut and sold, same being coarse and not fit food for the deer.' The gate probably takes its name from the charcoal which may once have been burnt near here and removed through it. It served the farm which stood within the park on the site of the present Kingsfarm Plantation.]

Robin Hood Gate: One of the six original gates. It was probably first called Wimbledon Gate, but by the mid-eighteenth century was already known as Robin Hood Gate on account of the proximity of the Robin Hood Inn. It was widened in 1907.

At the foot of Broomfield Hill note the patch of gorse protected by a railing, one of the few remnants of the extensive gorse cover when the park was enclosed. There are two other patches of gorse (i) between Conduit Wood and Holly (Bog) Lodge, and (ii) another fenced patch on the south side of Spankers Hill. Even a century ago there were large tracts of gorse in the enclosed preserves in the park, but once these were thrown open the gorse bushes were progressively eliminated, since the deer are partial to its young and tender shoots. Gorse forms an important refuge for wildlife.

At the top of Broomfield Hill, towards Ladderstile Gate, a section of wall was removed in the nineteenth century and replaced by a ha-ha, to afford a parkland vista following the construction of the Italianate Kingston Hill Place in 1828. On the north-east side of the ha-ha are traces of a bridle gate that existed in the mid-eighteenth century and seems to have been bricked up sometime in the nineteenth century. Lily Langtry lived here, but one must doubt that her friendship with Edward, Prince of Wales, which flourished in the 1880s, involved the White Lodge, since the Tecks were in residence there from 1869-1899.

Ladderstile Gate: one of the six original gates, it was known as Coombe Gate and provided access for the parishioners of Coombe (now commemorated in the name Coombe Lane running from Kingston to Raynes Park). During the first court action of 1754 the gate figured in the evidence. There had been both a gate and a stepladder. The gate had been locked in the early years of the century and actually bricked up in about 1735. Among the evidence produced in 1754 was the remarkable fact that

> 'Mr Hervey, late of Comb Park, was deprived of his key [to Ladderstile Gate] and in revenge planted French wheat in the adjacent lands, by which he enticed over the Pheasants, and killed ten brace in a day.'

The stepladder was reinstated after John Lewis' test case in 1758 and remained until about 1884, long after the other stepladders around the park had disappeared (except at Ham), hence it became popularly known as Ladderstile Gate about 1850. The present gate dates from 1901.

Ladderstile Gate had one moment of notoriety. At 3am on 17 April 1874 a desperate encounter took place between a local burglar, George Offord, and Police Constable Kerrison. Offord discharged a revolver at PC Kerrison before climbing up the ladderstile. Kerrison bravely pursued him but was struck over the head with the revolver butt. Despite serious head injuries Kerrison hung onto Offord's leg until help came and Offord was overpowered.

Ladderstile Cottage was built in the 1780s.

Kingston Gate: was not one of the original six park gates and only seems to have come into existence in about 1750. In 1861 Queen Victoria opened a new pair of iron gates, opened to foot passengers all night from 1877. The existing gate dates from 1898.

Ham Gate: One of the original six gates. The gate lodge, the only surviving original, was built in 1742. A ladderstile survived until 1850 or so. The present gate was widened in 1921 and the present wrought iron gates substituted for the previous wooden ones. Note the chinoiserie lantern lights over the gate installed in 1825, still lit by gas.

Follow the Sudbrook (just beyond Ham Gate Pond).

Note the ancient pollarded willows on its banks.

Skirt the edge of Sudbrook Park.

Most of Sudbrook Park had been acquired piecemeal by John, 2nd Duke of Argyll, but the lease of about 30 acres of the park was granted by George I in 1726. This made possible the construction by James Gibbs of the fine mansion across the old park boundary, visible across the present golf course, in 1728. Hence no wall exists along this stretch of the park perimeter. You will have seen Gibbs' work before – St Martin-in-the-Fields and St Mary-le-Strand in London, and closer to home the Octagon attached to Orleans House Gallery. Argyll's estate now extended up to Pembroke Lodge on the escarpment and abutted Petersham Park to the north. A few bricks and stones are all that remain of a small reservoir halfway up the hill, which used to supply Sudbrook Park with water. Part of the Sudbrook estate subsequently reverted to the Crown and was reintegrated into the park. The golf club was established in 1891.

Petersham Gate: A large ornamental gate served Petersham Lodge from 1686. After Petersham Park was reintegrated into the Richmond Park in 1833, a pedestrian gate replaced it, which served the Russell School (see Walk No.9). The carriage gate a few metres up the hill was probably the tradesmen's access to the school, or was once access to the stables of Petersham Lodge. Halfway up Star and Garter Hill, there is a permanently locked foot gate. There is also a stretch of wall where the brickwork was replaced by railings in 1843, nine years after the reincorporation of Petersham Park, to provide a vista onto Petersham Common from the terrace walk above. At the time Petersham Common would have been much more open, almost certainly wood pasture, with grazing livestock and enticing glimpses of the river below.

Richmond Gate: is one of the original six gates and seems always to have borne the heaviest traffic. The present gate and lodge bearing the cyphers GR (George III) and CR (his consort Queen Charlotte) was erected in 1798, almost certainly to a design

Richmond Gate, with its ladderstile, c.1750. Note the summer house on the right, also marked on Eyre's map, p.86. It looks like the same site marked 'The Arbour' on Lane's enclosure map in 1637.

by Sir John Soane (original drawings in the Soane Museum, Lincoln's Inn Fields). The gates were widened in 1896. According to a guide book dated 1824:

> 'Large iron gates open to receive carriages into its domains. Upon ringing a bell and producing an order from the deputy ranger, Lord Sidmouth, the keeper at the lodge, remarkable for his civility, appears for your admission.'

Princess Amelia would have been mortified.

Beside Richmond Gate stands Ancaster House, now the residence of the Commandant of the Star and Garter Home. It was built in 1772 by the Duke of Ancaster. It was then acquired by a baronet, Sir Lionel Darell. Darell found the park wall oppressively close to his house and wanted a larger garden. How he succeeded illustrates perfectly that it is *who* you know not what you know that counts. At first he went through all the correct channels, applying to the Lords of the Treasury and the Commissioners of Crown Lands, to no avail since both offices found one reason after another to demur and delay. Ever had that feeling? Always go to the top. When George III was riding past one day and bade him good day, Darell seized his chance. 'How much do you want?' asked the king. When Darell showed him his modest intentions, the king expostulated, 'Are you sure that will be enough? Don't stint yourself.' Fortunately for us Darell did not have the presence of mind to request another 50 acres. George dismounted and marked out a line himself with a stick, saying 'There you are, that is your ground, it is mine no longer.' Hence Darell removed the wall, and railings mark his slightly enlarged garden.

Bishop's (Chisholm Road) **Gate**: previously consisting of two large wooden gates. The Cattle Gate, as it used to be known, was for livestock allowed to pasture in the park in the nineteenth century.

It was not opened to the public until 1896, as a result of a petition from those living in Chisholm Road and nearby. Bishop's Gate is one of the only places where one may still see the 16.5ft freebord of Crown property that runs (invisibly) around most of the park. It is the dogleg through to Chisholm Road.

Bishop's Lodge, built into the wall at Bishop's Gate towards the end of the eighteenth century, was probably named after two assistant keepers, William Bishop and his son Charles, employed between 1790-1830, approximately.

Cambrian Road Gate: This, the youngest gate, was constructed for the convenience of the South Africa Military Hospital (Walk No.9) during the First World War. When the latter was demolished in 1925, the entrance was made permanent and public as a cradle gate.

The Park in the nineteenth century

In spite of winning the battle for public access in 1758, pedestrians were still expected to keep to the footpaths, and carriages were required to obtain admission cards until the 1850s. The map below, produced in 1876, indicates that even after visitors were encouraged to enjoy the park, substantial portions of the park were still designated as Preserves, or for special use.

Yet Richmond Park did begin to change, ceasing to be a hunting park and becoming more of a pleasurable place to promenade. This was largely due to two men, Lord Sidmouth and Edward Jesse. As mentioned in the preceding walk, in 1813 George III (the first monarch to hold the Rangership personally) made Sidmouth his Deputy Ranger, effectively his park manager. Sidmouth, already at the White Lodge, dined Walter Scott, Pitt the Younger, Richard Sheridan, who lived at Downe House on the Terrace, and most notably Lord Nelson, who apparently dipped his finger in his wine glass to trace out his battle plan for destroying the French fleet on the dining table at White Lodge, a manoeuvre duly executed the following year at Trafalgar.

Sidmouth conceived a passion for trees and initiated a programme of tree planting that continued throughout the century long after his death in 1844. How far the park had become depleted of trees is difficult to say, and it may be that all Sidmouth and his successors did was to ensure the park remained amply stocked. But from Sidmouth onwards, tree planting became a central consideration in administration of the park, with major plantings in the 1820s and 1830s, and again in the 1870s and 1880s. Most of the plantations were fenced in to protect them from the deer, the fences only removed after Edward VII's

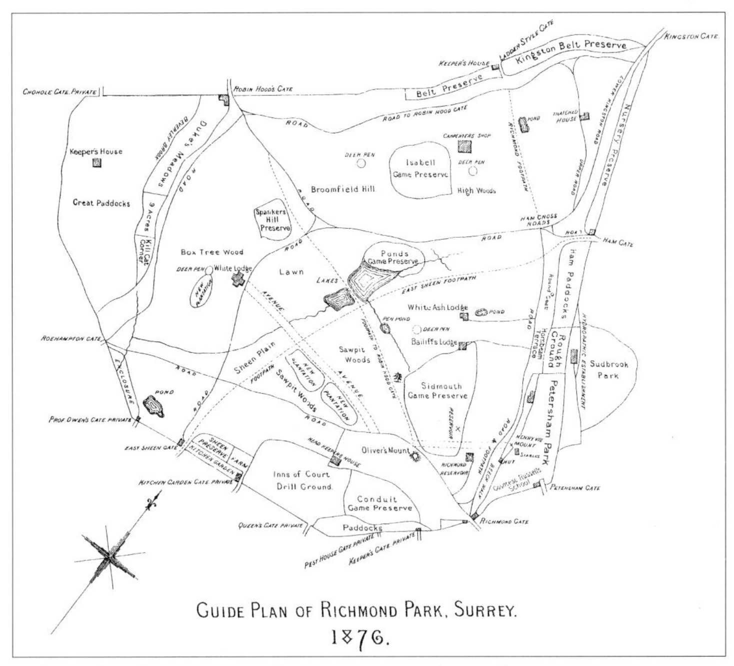

Richmond Park in 1876. Note the compass points due south.

decision in 1906 to make all parts of the park accessible to the public. Sidmouth also preferred sessile oak (*Quercus petraea*) to pedunculate oak, on the grounds that it was more adaptable to different soil conditions. One may wonder at this, given the evidence of so many pedunculate oaks here, successfully entering their sixth or even seventh century.

Sidmouth himself had had two priorities, to create a number of closely planted woods in the body of the park and also to conceal much of the park perimeter behind trees. Perhaps he anticipated the urbanisation that took place around the perimeter from about 1850 onwards.

The nineteenth century short walk

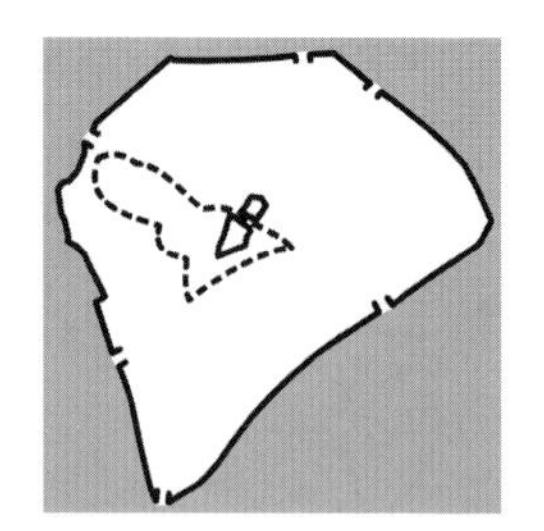

Distance 6km: 1.5 hours

If you wish to walk further, Walk No 8 provides a longer version.

Start at the Pen Ponds Car Park.

Sidmouth started in 1819 by planting a section of trees on Spanker's Hill on the east side of the car park, above and behind the Old Lodge which was still standing. This plantation was enlarged in 1824, and again in 1877.

Between the car park and the Upper Pen Pond lies Lawn Plantation, one of the last 19th century plantations (1883), and a good example of some of the smaller tree clusters subsequently planted. ('Lawn' or 'laund', incidentally, is old English for a stretch of untilled ground or a woodland clearing.)

Proceed westwards along the road towards Ham Cross.

On your right the south-west end of the Pen Pond, Pond Plantation, was planted in 1865. It remains fenced as a waterfowl preserve. On your right, Isabella Plantation, planted from 1831, is also still fenced, to protect its woodland garden from the deer (see Walk No.11).

After almost 1 km turn right at the cross paths at the end of Pen Pond Plantation, crossing Pond Slade.

Besides Lord Sidmouth, the other nineteenth century figure of note was the naturalist Edward Jesse, Surveyor of HM Parks and Palaces, who recorded his observations of Richmond Park in his *Gleanings of Natural History* (London, 1834-35). Jesse's two major contributions concerned the quality of the land and the size of the park. Jesse was anxious to increase venison production, and in a survey in 1831 he recommended yet another major effort be made to drain the boggy areas of the park in order to provide better grazing. There had been numerous attempts in the past to drain boggy areas, notably the works carried out by Edward Manning at the time of the enclosure, and by George III at the end of the eighteenth century. Jesse's recommendation was not immediately implemented, no doubt because previous efforts had been so unsuccessful. Two areas were particularly wet, Pond Slade, which you are now crossing, and the area north and north east of Holly (Bog) Lodge.

Jesse's recommendation was revived in the 1850s because of the spreading fame of a new drainage expert, Josiah Parkes (1793-1871). Traditionally land drains were relatively shallow, in the belief that achieving good run-off would ensure that the land would not become waterlogged. Parkes, however, had noticed that his experimental deep drains began to run after wet weather not from the water above but from the water rising from subterranean accumulation below, and that by draining the stagnant moisture from 4 foot below the surface, the soil was rendered more friable and porous. In 1856 he was commissioned to design and implement a system of drains for about three quarters of the park, a job completed in 1861, together with the construction of nine new ponds (listed on p.187) as watering for the deer. Parkes' work was largely successful. The land became better drained, leading to improved pasture for the deer herds but a diminished natural environment. Ensuring satisfactory land drains remained a perennial task until the 1990s when it was decided that intensive drainage impoverished the park ecology, and that retention of the park's natural wetness was desirable. Currently the policy is to allow many of these drains progressively to silt up, with some areas reverting to a boggy condition. This will have the added advantage of deterring all but the determined from walking through it, thereby encouraging wildlife.

Take the path forking left after 200m and make for White Ash Lodge, go round the back of it and follow its drive out to the main carriageway. Cross the carriageway and 75m on opposite side turn right into the Hornbeam Walk (glance to your left to enjoy the vista of the Walk).

The Hornbeam Walk was probably planted in the 1840s, a deliberate move in the conversion of the park from a place of desperate chases into one for pleasant promenades. Put a stethoscope to a hornbeam trunk in spring and one will apparently hear the pulse of the rising sap, louder than in any other native tree species. Note Oak Lodge on your right (half hidden in the southern corner of Sidmouth Plantation) built in the early 1850s to accommodate the park bailiff, responsible for general maintenance of the park.

At the end of the Hornbeam Walk (200m) enter Pembroke Lodge grounds through the wicket gate, walk round to the terrace overlooking the Thames Valley.

This is a suitable moment for a small historical diversion. It will be recalled from Walk No.5 that Lord John Russell (1792-1878) moved into Pembroke Lodge in 1847. Russell had made his name championing the passage of the Reform Bill of 1832. He came from an aristocratic family (the dukes of Bedford) noted for its public spirit. His own liberal inclinations were probably also due to a private education rather than attendance at a public school and, eschewing Oxbridge, his attendance at Edinburgh University where he imbibed the philosophy of the Scottish Enlightenment. He championed the cause of religious freedom for English Dissenters and Irish Catholics, but as prime minister his attempts to end civil disabilities for Jews, extend the franchise to urban workers and guarantee security of tenure to Irish farmers were all frustrated by party disunity. Thwarted in public life, he retreated to Pembroke Lodge where he wrote copiously – poetry, biography and history – till his death.

Pembroke Lodge was also the childhood home of his grandson, Bertrand Russell. He arrived at the age of four, and the opening sentence of his autobiography reads 'My first vivid recollection is my arrival at Pembroke Lodge in February 1876.' He had come to Pembroke Lodge because both parents died before he was four. His parents were unconventional. They had appointed a naturalist and atheist, Douglas Alexander Spalding, as tutor for Bertrand's older brother. (Spalding, incidentally had anticipated Konrad Lorenz's discovery of 'imprinting' [through the study of ducks and geese] by more than 60 years.) Bertrand's parents, Lord and Lady Amberley, thought that as a consumptive, Spalding should remain childless. But, being liberals, this created a moral dilemma, for they thought 'it was unfair to expect him to be celibate,' as Bertrand wrote in his autobiography. Only generous behaviour towards Spalding would do: 'My mother therefore, allowed him to live with her, thought I know of no evidence that she derived any pleasure from doing so.' Equally, there is no evidence that she did not. But whatever the pleasure on either side, it did not last long. She died in 1874, followed in 1876 by her husband. But before he expired he appointed Spalding as one of Bertrand Russell's guardians, perhaps another generous gesture, this time to satisfy any paternal desires he may have had.

However, when Lord and Lady Russell got wind both of their daughter-in-law's sexual liberalism and of Spalding's atheism, they intervened to protect the children, who became the wards of their grandmother, Lady Russell, a woman of strict personal conscience and Puritan views. Whatever Bertrand lost in a liberal education, he gained in the joy he found in the garden here and he more than made up for his grandmother's illiberal views later on in life. Indeed, she would have had a fit.

> 'Throughout the greater part of my childhood, the most important hours of my day were those that I spent in the garden. I knew each corner of the garden, and looked year by year for the white primroses in one place, the redstart's nest in another, the blossom of the acacia emerging from a tangle of ivy. I knew where the earliest bluebells were to be found, and which of the oaks came into leaf soonest ...'

One of his great childhood friends was Annabel Grant Duff, who lived at York House, Twickenham. In a memoir of her early life, she wrote:

> 'My only boy friend was Bertrand Russell. Bertie and I were great allies and I had a secret admiration for his beautiful and gifted elder brother Frank. Frank, I am sorry to say, sympathized with my brother's point of view about little girls and used to tie me up to trees by my hair. But Bertie, a solemn little boy in a blue velvet suit with an equally solemn governess, was always kind, and I greatly enjoyed going to tea at Pembroke Lodge. But even as a child I realized what

an unsuitable place it was for children to be brought up in. Lady Russell always spoke in hushed tones and Lady Agatha always wore a white shawl and looked down-trodden.... They all drifted in and out of the rooms like ghosts and no one ever seemed to be hungry. It was a curious bringing up for two young and extraordinarily gifted boys.'

Educated privately, Russell became intensely interested, in his own words, in 'how much we can be said to know and with what degree of certainty or doubtfulness.' The rest, as they say, is history, as he became internationally celebrated as philosopher, pacifist and campaigner against nuclear weaponry. In the prologue to his autobiography, he wrote:

'Three passions, simple but overwhelmingly strong, have governed my life: the longing for love, the search for knowledge, and unbearable pity for the suffering of mankind.'

Nice to think – in spite of Annabel Grant Duff's assessment – of Pembroke Lodge as the cradle for such greatness.

And now back to earth.

Descend from the terrace and turn right out of the gate at the bottom of the garden. You are now walking along the old perimeter of Petersham Park.

It will be recalled from Walk No.4 that Charles II had granted the Petersham section of the park along with the Keepership to the Countess of Dysart (hence the eponymous Petersham pub); that in 1683 the Earl of Rochester had been granted a personal lease over a 50 acre plot, and that his magnificent mansion, 'New Park', had been destroyed by fire in 1721; that eleven years later Lord Burlington had designed a new lodge for Lord Harrington. By the end of the eighteenth century the property, now about 100 acres in size, was in the hands of Lord Huntingtower (another

Dysart descendant). This large estate stretched all the way from the park wall at the bottom of the hill up to Pembroke Lodge and the fence running along the escarpment to Richmond Gate.

Jesse, as Surveyor of HM Parks, had had his eye on Petersham Park and when Lord Huntingtower died in 1833 he persuaded his principals to buy Petersham Park for £14,500 and reintegrate it into Richmond Park. Petersham Lodge, already virtually derelict, was demolished in 1835. Trees of the parkland (or their descendants) still festoon the hillside, including old cedars (Lebanon, Atlantic and Deodar) then probably only seedlings. For the Russell school, which stood beside Petersham Gate, see Walk No.9.

Proceed along the western (just under the escarpment) edge of Pembroke Lodge Grounds for about 600m, pass on your right a nineteenth century brick-domed artesian well-house. Continue until steps bring you back onto the escarpment.

At the top you will cross the end of Jesse's 'New Terrace' or Beech Walk. This is less successful than the Hornbeam Walk, but was intended to provide a pleasant walk (where none had previously existed) from Richmond Gate to Pembroke Lodge with splendid views across the recently re-integrated Petersham parkland. Jesse had many of the trees cleared from Petersham Park and from the old boundary fence in order to provide a view of the river from the Beech Walk. It was also at about this time that railings replaced the wall on Star and Garter Hill in order to give a view across Petersham Meadow. These views have now been lost due to foliage growth. Furthermore, while some beeches have been replanted the walk now lacks the coherence one suspects was originally intended.

Cross the Richmond-Kingston carriageway and turn right along the horsetrack. When the horsetrack begins to veer back towards the carriageway, strike off straight ahead, through the last trees of Kidney Wood. As you approach Sidney Wood, note a raised area with manhole covers.

This is a covered reservoir, one of two built in 1875-76, with Queen Victoria's consent, to supply Richmond with pumped Thames water. In 1860 Richmond had agreed to the supply of water by Southwark and Vauxhall Water Company, in spite of its relatively high prices. In 1873 S&V doubled its prices for water that proved to be badly polluted, and it was decided to replace its expensive services with locally supplied water. With this in mind two reservoirs were constructed (the other is in Sidmouth Wood, just behind the section of feather-edged fencing opposite Pembroke Lodge car park). S&V refused to allow its own mains network to be used, an exercise of hard-nosed capitalism in the face of community need. Before the reservoirs were finished or houses re-connected, S&V cut off its supply in January 1877. For a month water was brought into Richmond mainly by water-bowser, a major source of water being Leg of Mutton Pond (still then known as the Pen Pond, between Sidmouth Wood and the Pen Ponds), which produced purer water, so it was claimed, than S&V.

Follow the edge of Sidmouth Wood southwards 200m to the wicket gate leading into the Driftway.

Sidmouth's best memorial, of course, is the wood named after him. The north-western tip was planted in 1823 and the rest in 1830. The vista through the avenue of trees from King

Henry VIII's mound was preserved as a cutting through the plantation (to be admired on Walk No.1). During the third quarter of the nineteenth century the wood was used as a pheasant cover. The Driftway itself was only opened to the public in 1906. The nineteenth century introduction of rhododendron, of course, was not in the ecological interest of the wood, where brambles or native coppice would have been very much preferable for birds and mammals.

On emerging from the Driftway veer around the northern tip of the dark and forbidding Queen Elizabeth's Plantation, past the Leg of Mutton Pond, (admiring but preferably not testing its potable quality) back to the Pen Pond car park.

The nineteenth century long walk

Distance 9km: 2.5 hours

This is an extended version of Walk No.7.

Start at Sheen Wood car park (East Sheen Gate).

Sheen Wood, along with Spanker's Hill Wood, the first of Lord Sidmouth's plantations, was the beginning of his plan to obscure much of the park wall. In 1825 he planted trees from Sheen Cottage, 200m east of East Sheen Gate (see Walk No.9), to Roehampton Gate, and the following year trees along the wall from Kingston Vale over the hill to Kingston Gate. At the same time he planted more trees along Ham Bottom from Kingston Gate to Ham Gate.

Walk towards Roehampton Gate following the plantation, but turn southwards when you reach Beverley Brook and make for the woods behind (east of) The White Lodge.

White Lodge Wood is representative of the 1870s programme intended to thicken up thinly wooded areas. This area was originally planted when cultivation was abandoned, probably in the fourteenth century. At the time of the enclosure it was known as 'Slawood', which possibly referred to a mire at the foot of the slope. The wooden deer pen on the north-east slopes of

White Lodge wood is the only one surviving from the nineteenth century. There was originally a smaller pen inside that could only be entered by fawns/calves. This was to ensure they obtained sufficient supplementary food.

Continue walking due south through Treebox Wood (1877) and around the east and southern side of Spankers Hill Wood.

Spanker's Hill Wood was planted between 1819-24, around Hartleton (The Old) Lodge, which was still standing.

Pass the Pen Ponds car park on your right and follow Walk No 7, until you have walked through the Sidmouth Wood Driftway and emerged on the south east side. Now turn left (but not hard left) and walk 500m across the hillside, crossing the major path running down to the Pen Ponds, until you reach the Queen's Ride.

At the west end of the Queen's Ride, close to the tenth tree on its northern side, there is a Mortlake Parish boundary stone dated 1867. It is difficult to spot. In theory there are several other parish boundary stones in the park, but they all seem to have been buried under detritus.

Walk down the Queen's Ride, skirt around Saw Pit Plantation, and turn northwards, back to Sheen Cross, and thence back to Sheen Wood car park.

The Park in the twentieth century

It may seem surprising in an age of self-conscious conservation that the park underwent greater changes during the twentieth century than in any preceding one. This was as much because of the decision by Edward VII to develop the park as a public amenity, as because of the two disruptive world wars. Edward VII ordered the opening of virtually all the previously fenced woods, the only substantial exceptions being Sidmouth Wood (but public access to the Driftway was established), Pond Plantation (as a bird sanctuary) and Teck Plantation near East Sheen Gate, and private gates were made public for the benefit of the greatly increased local population. It was the act of an increasingly 'middle class' monarchy for the demanding and predominantly middle class suburbs. In this respect at any rate, George V followed faithfully in his father's footsteps. From 1915 level areas

The London Scottish marching into camp, 1915.

of the park were marked out for football and cricket pitches, presumably for the troops as well as local clubs. No less than 40 such pitches existed by 1939. In 1923 the golf course was opened by the Prince of Wales for those – in fact 'local artisans' – who could not afford membership of a private club, another example of the new popular monarchy.

The effects of world war were threefold: military camps and hospitals were constructed in the park; over a quarter of the park was either put under cultivation (mainly around East Sheen Gate) or used as grazing; and certain buildings were destroyed by enemy action. F. D. Ommaney, who spent his youth in Sheen Cottage (see below) recalled of the First War:

> 'Every holiday, when I returned home, the ugly evidences of war spread farther and wider over the green spaces around the house in the park. For several centuries it had looked out upon scenes of immemorial peace. Now, from the warlike clamour that increased around it, it seemed to shrink back among the trees. Rows of huts sprang up and the inevitable cookhouses and latrines accompanied them. Guns pushed up their snouts among the trees. Army lorries, disregarding the sacred rules enforced upon us for years by stately old gentlemen in top hats with gold braid around them [the park police], careered across the green levels and scarred them with their wheels. In the plantations they stood in rows like prehistoric monsters asleep. Captive balloons hung above, obese shapes in our familiar sky. Columns of soldiers marched and drilled, attracting from the purlieus down the hill troops of raffish *vivandières*, who wandered about in groups and made sly giggling invitations. The sound of rifle fire and bursting grenades echoed among the copses.'

Scout cars of GHQ (Phantom) Liaison Regiment put through their paces on the slope below Thatched House Lodge.

During the Second World War the Pen Ponds themselves were drained to disguise so prominent a landmark, and not refilled until 1948.

The remarkable fact is that at the end of the century, apart from the loss of pre-war buildings, it is only an informed eye that will detect where these activities were. Most traces have been carefully erased. The real transformation of the park from the Arcadian retreat it once was results from the relentless traffic crossing it during the daylight hours, the noise of aircraft approaching or leaving Heathrow Airport and heavy foot traffic and dogs off established paths. All seriously diminish the quality of Richmond Park, certainly as a place for wildlife.

Richmond Park was also the scene of wartime innovation. In November 1917 trials were carried out on H. G. Wells' 'aerial ropeway'. Far from being a batty brainstorm, Wells had evolved this way of moving rations, ammunition, equipment and wounded men, following the death of hundreds of men carrying rations and ammunition up to the front line in the Third Battle of Ypres. Some had died under enemy fire, others had slipped off the duckboards and drowned in flooded shell craters. Wells' ropeway was designed to be erected after dark for night use. It was hung on 10' poles and could convey 10 tons per hour for a distance of half a mile. But the generals turned it down. Wells commented, 'the tin hats did not like it', bitterly deriding them as 'fine, handsome, well-groomed, neighing gentlemen' with 'clear definite ideas of what war was.'

In the Second World War, the park was used for special forces. GHQ (Phantom) Liaison Regt trained here, the actor David Niven among them. The regiment suffered 50 per cent casualties, for they were used as scouts to locate the enemy. During the retreat to Dunkirk it is unkindly said they spent more time trying to find the French than the enemy. Some personnel were used as 'listeners' either forward of the front line or parachuted behind enemy lines to eavesdrop on German wireless transmissions.

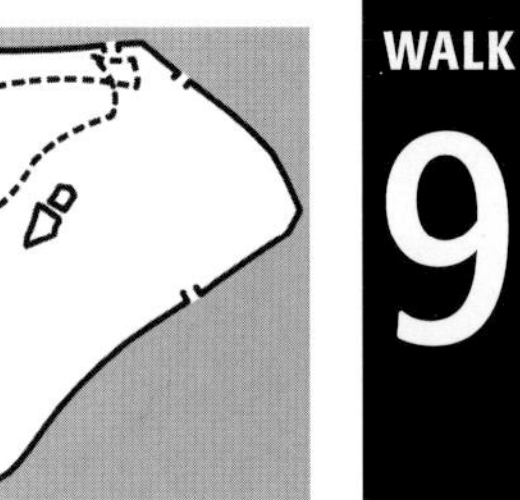

The twentieth century walk

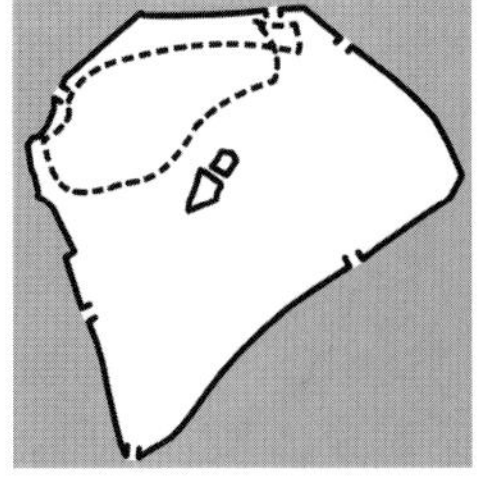

Distance 6.5km: 1.5 hours or 11km: 2.5 hours

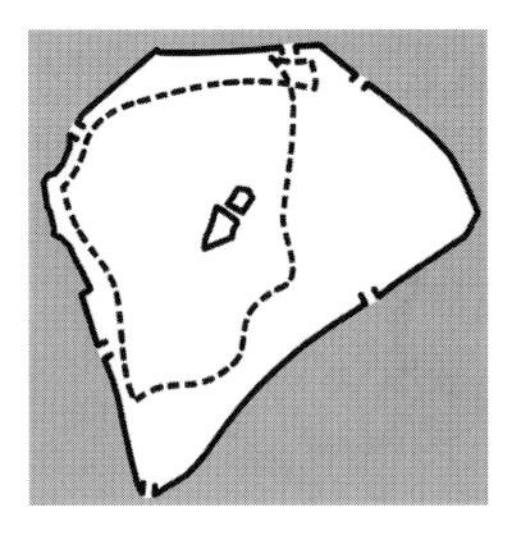

Start at Sheen Wood car park (East Sheen Gate). Turn east (left) and walk 150m along the wall.

Traces of Sheen Cottage are discernible on the park wall, which has been extensively patched. It was originally built against the park wall probably in the 1720s by Sir Robert Walpole for his huntsman and deerhounds, and was marked on eighteenth century maps simply as 'Dog Kennel'. With the end of deer hunting in the middle of the century the house was occupied by one of the park under-keepers. But in about 1787 a William Adam obtained permission to occupy part of the house, and then paid the under-keeper compensation to vacate the whole property. Adam, who became High Commissioner for Scotland during George IV's reign, his son, who became Accountant General of the Court of Chancery, and then his two grandsons, all occupied the house until 1852. The house was enlarged along the wall. It had one garden inside the park and another outside it. It is from Adam that the nearby pond derives its name.

Sir Richard Owen (1804-92), eminent anatomist, palaeontologist and first Director of the Natural History Museum, was the

Sheen Cottage.

next occupant of Sheen Cottage, until his death. In the words of his great grandson, F. D. Ommaney:

> 'He expounded the manners and habits of beasts ... his wife ... recorded ... how he brought back the remains of a hippopotamus from the Zoo to dissect at home, filling the house with too-African odours. A faint note of protest was perceptible in the patient diary ...
>
> 'The old man lived in this house until he died at a great age – over ninety. He ... was a dominating and masterful spirit with great personal charm, which he could turn on and off like a tap, and a biting sarcastic humour which he apparently reserved for his large family circle.'

Owen was the foremost natural scientist of his day and his classification of fossils became the basic reference for the rest of the century. Nevertheless, from the 1850s he came under increasing attack from a younger generation of scientists who looked beyond Britain to the work and theories of German scientists and, in Thomas Huxley's words, he became 'both feared and hated'. Yet the real body blow for Owen came from a friend, Charles Darwin. Darwin's theory of natural selection put an axe at the very roots of Owen's own theoretical basis. It was all the harder to take since he, Owen, was a professional anatomist, while Darwin was essentially an amateur. Where he had meticulously sifted his evidence, bone by bone in the laboratory, Darwin had gallivanted off to look at living creatures. Deeply threatened, Owen anonymously attacked the *Origin of Species,* following its publication in 1859. Darwin responded:

> 'It is extremely malignant, clever, and I fear will be very damaging.. It requires much study to appreciate all the bitter spite of many of the remarks against me... He misquotes some passages, altering words within inverted commas...'

You may still find traces of the old building and garden, the highlight of your researches being the site of the household's flush lavatory. It was destroyed, the cottage that is, by enemy action in 1944.

Pick up the riding track just south of Adam's Pond and follow it westwards, past Holly (Bog) Lodge to Bishop's Pond (2km).

Virtually the whole area between Conduit Wood and Bishop's Pond was the site of the South Africa Military Hospital, built during the First World War close to Cambrian Road, where the park wall was pierced to allow access (see Walk No.6). The hospital extended over 12 acres, and was composed of rows of wooden huts on brick piers, designed 'after the manner of South African colonial timber-framed dwellings'. One may easily imagine the horse drawn ambulances making their laborious way up from Richmond Station with their pain-wracked loads.

Main entrance to the South African War Hospital. Below: the hospital layout.

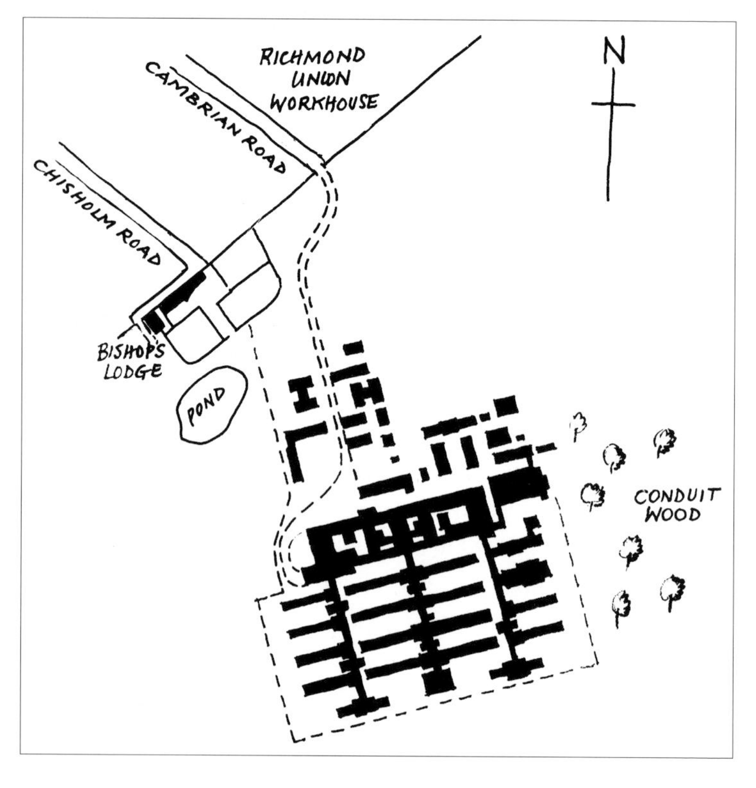

The hospital facilities were said to be the most advanced of their kind in Britain, and included 'bath beds' – the only ones of their kind in Britain – for those with bad shell wounds or advanced septicaemia. The patient would recline on a cradle suspended in flowing water at body temperature. This treatment, normally lasting 4-5 days, greatly eased the pain otherwise incurred by changing dressings, helped drain septic wounds and made sleep easier. However, the South African Forces section of Richmond Cemetery bears melancholy testimony to the large number of young men who failed to make it – a powerful reminder of the pity of war.

The hospital was assigned to the Ministry of Pensions at the end of the war and only demolished in 1925. During dry summer weather one can still see the outline of the earthworks connected with the hospital on the ground used as an informal football pitch.

Walk to Richmond Gate, and follow the wall down to Petersham Gate (1 km).

The Russell School stood beside the gate, at the very foot of the hill. It was established by Lady Russell of Pembroke Lodge (see Walk No.7) in a room in Petersham in 1849 and two years later moved into the new building just inside Petersham Gate. The new schoolhouse contained three classrooms, for infants, middles and seniors which, as one ex-pupil recalled, '... sloped steeply to the back, with steps which tripped the unwary'. In the summer most lessons took place under the cedar trees, the park itself being 'our delight ... the most perfect of all playgrounds'. The schoolhouse was destroyed by enemy action in 1943. It was rebuilt on the Petersham Road. Nothing remains of the original school.

The Russell School in the late nineteenth century.

To return to East Sheen Gate: proceed through Petersham Park, climbing back on to the escarpment at the south end of Pembroke Lodge, skirting the south side of Sidmouth Wood, across the Queen's Ride, through Sawpit Plantation, and past Barn Wood Pond (3.5km);

OR

If you are feeling energetic, continue walking through Petersham Park and Ham Bottom, climbing the escarpment on the south side of Thatched House Lodge (2.5km). (This part may be done as a separate outing from Kingston or Ladderstile Gates, or Broomfield Hill Car park).

You are now on the edge of Kingston Gate Camp, an army hutted camp established in 1938 to house conscripts of the East Surrey Regiment. It was subsequently used as a military convalescent depot, then by the women's army unit, the Auxiliary

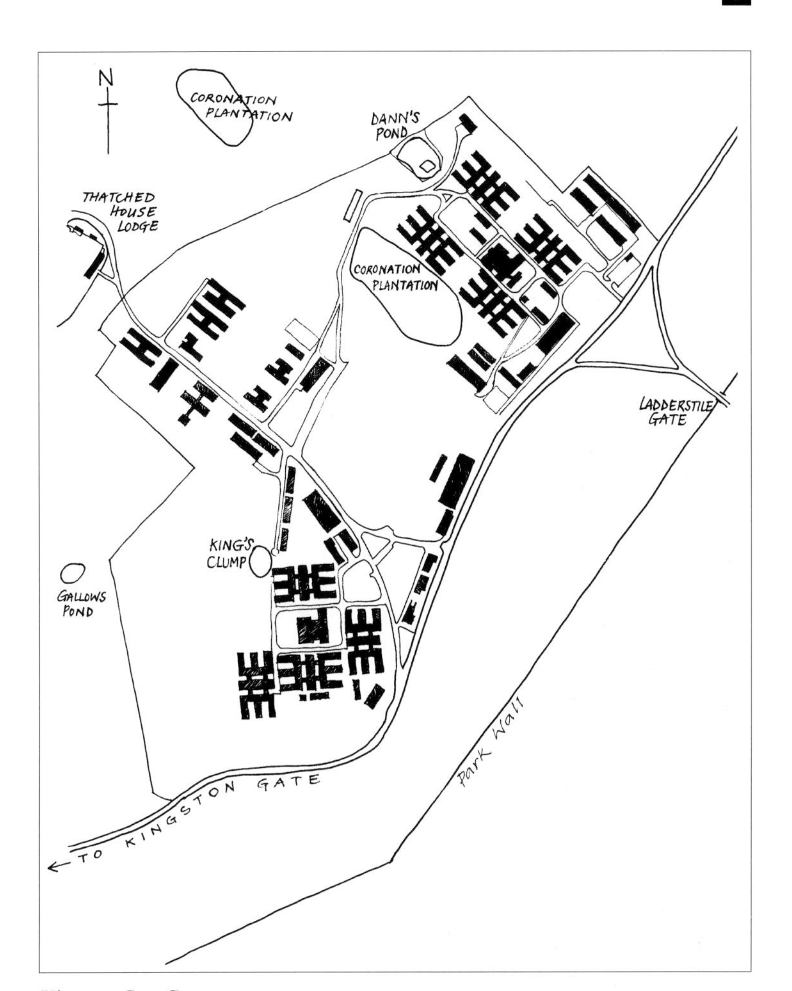

Kingston Gate Camp.

Territorial Service (ATS) and after the war by its successor unit, the Women's Royal Army Corps (WRAC). It was used as an extremely cramped and spartan Olympic Village in 1948, and as a hostel for service families evacuated from the Suez Canal Zone in 1956. It was dismantled in 1965 and re-integrated into the park in the summer of 1966. There are plenty of people around who remember it. It was extensive, occupying an area on the northern side of the Kingston - Robin Hood Gate carriageway from Dark Hill/King's Clump, across to Thatched House Lodge, and up to Dann's Pond. One can still see earthworks including the covered remains of a tennis court just east of Thatched House Lodge. The only surviving surface evidence of the camp is a (now meaningless) flight of eight concrete steps (if you can find them).

Follow the track past Dann's Pond, and around the south east side of Isabella Plantation (Walk No.11) and go through the cutting across Prince Charles' Spinney.

There were already some trees here, but the spinney was planted in 1951, three years after Prince Charles' birth. A spinney implies a grove of thorn trees, and the handful of hawthorns here barely justifies the name.

Emerge from the spinney and bear left, pass Pen Ponds car park, and follow the carriageway back past the White Lodge and East Sheen Gate (or if you have made this a separate walk, return to your start point.)

Richmond Parish boundary

WALK 10

Distance 2km: 40 minutes

BEFORE YOU WALK

Visible traces of the old manorial and parish boundaries are meagre. A pattern of parishes, the ecclesiastical administration of England, was well established by 1000AD. Most parish boundaries, even in the remoter parts of England had been drawn by the end of the twelfth century. By the fifteenth century there were some 10,000 parishes in England and theoretically these became units of civil administration rather than solely ecclesiastical units in the sixteenth century.

Yet in practice the medieval manor remained a more important unit of administration until well into the seventeenth century. As noted in Walk No.4, leases and holdings were still recorded in terms of manor boundaries, and these are what were marked on maps of the time. They were often coterminous with the parish boundaries.

However, the tradition of 'beating the parish bounds' every Ascension Day had already been established by the reign of Elizabeth I, from older ceremonies of Rogationtide. Although originally a religious ceremony, beating the bounds had two functions: to ensure that the boundaries of the parish had not been infringed and if so, to challenge that infringement (as is clear from the incident of 1751 described in Walk No.6) and to instil in the minds of all villagers, particularly the young, the exact limits of the parish. The parson would lead his parishioners around the boundary in procession, stopping at certain oak trees to offer prayers for good crops (thus known as 'gospel oaks'). Some oaks were planted specifically as boundary marks, particularly where the boundary suddenly changed direction. Elsewhere stones were used. Most of these boundaries have been amended at least once in the intervening period since the sixteenth century. However, although parishes gave way to boroughs as units of administration (Richmond in 1890, for example), Ordnance Survey maps published earlier this century still showed oak trees that marked parish boundaries some of which must still be standing but, the bark having grown over their distinguishing marks, are now extraordinarily difficult to identify. One of the only surviving parish boundary stones (on the Mortlake-Petersham border) is easily located (Walk No.8, on p.128).

The Richmond Parish boundary is clearly marked – look for 'Richmond Common' – on Lane's map, p.64, and may easily be followed. You will be following a boundary that probably dates from before the Norman Conquest, to the Saxon establishment of the manors of Mortlake and Kingston, well before the first records of Shene as a manor separate from Kingston.

Enter the park at Richmond Gate.

The old boundary with Petersham enters the park just on the right, behind the public lavatories at the point where railings replace the full height park wall on Star and Garter Hill, and runs almost straight to the convex curve of the north-western edge of Sidmouth Wood.

Begin walking along the east side of the Richmond-Kingston carriageway.

Almost immediately there is large old oak (100 paces from the roundabout) probably a marker oak on the old parish boundary line.

Strike off slightly to the left of the carriageway and walk through the middle of Kidney Wood and make for the concave NW edge of Sidmouth wood.

The left hand wooden bench on the track skirting Sidmouth Wood is approximately where a large boundary oak stood 150 years ago, marking the apex of the wedge of Richmond parish common land falling within the park, and where the parishes of Petersham, Richmond and Mortlake met.

Turn east-north-east and start walking towards Conduit Wood following the lowest ground as it begins to become a gully, and then an open stream leading through the heart of Conduit Wood.

Of course, before the land was drained, the surface stream must have started close to Sidmouth Wood. One only has to think for a moment about the landscape in the eleventh century to realize that an obvious way to avoid territorial disputes between one manor and another upon a relatively empty landscape was to follow natural features. Hence the course of the stream here. Mortlake manor, belonging to the Archbishops of Canterbury, lay on the other side of the stream.

Follow the stream through the wood, out the far side.

On the edge of the boggy area 75m below Conduit Wood, one may find a half-buried stone outcrop which may be the remains of another pre-enclosure conduit house (see Walk No.4 for the White Conduit, the brick structure in Conduit Wood).

The stream turns left for the last 200 metres or so before reaching the park wall. This can be seen quite distinctly on Lane's map and appears to mark one side of Humphry Bennet's holding. Note the willows on the right bank, which are planted in straight lines along what may have been drainage ditches. It is unclear how long they have been there, but they indicate a field boundary at least 150 years old.

Just on the left of the culvert where the stream leaves the park, the wall is now patched. On either side of the stream stands a native black poplar (see p.99), one of them sadly truncated.

OTHER BOUNDARIES

Unfortunately other boundaries are much harder to follow:

1. MORTLAKE-PETERSHAM boundary ran from the north edge of Sidmouth Wood where there is a Mortlake boundary stone hidden in the rhododendrons just inside the metal fence, across to the west end of Sawpit Plantation. A boundary stone may be found, marked 'MP [Mortlake Parish] 1867', standing beside the tenth tree on the north side of the Queen's Ride. The boundary ran to another stone now buried in the bracken on the hill overlooking the Lower Pen Pond and then in a straight line down to the pond. At this point it became the boundary between Mortlake and Ham.

2. The MORTLAKE-HAM boundary crossed the Lower Pen Pond, and curved over the saddle between Spanker's and White Lodge hills to skirt the northern edge of Treebox Wood. This last section is traceable.

If you wish to find it, walk from Robin Hood Gate car park and walk downstream along Beverley Brook for about 500m until you reach the bridge to a metal gate letting onto the golf course. With your back to the bridge, walk towards the carriageway. The causeway is the old Mortlake-Ham boundary. Cross the carriageway and walk 75m up the rough track leading into Treebox Wood. On your right you should see a ditch and bank (29) running off at an angle. This then runs up the northern edge of Treebox Wood, a few paces north of the tree line, and is traceable up to the brow of the hill.

The boundary along this stretch coincides with the northern boundary of Prior's Hill Copse marked on Lane's map. The southern boundary of Prior's Hill Copse, incidentally, may also be identified, since it runs along the line of bracken (**31**) on the edge of the open greensward stretching back towards the car park (see sketch map), and may more or less be traced as a slight bank back to the edge of the round pond in Spanker's Hill Wood. While retracing your steps to the car park, the south-east boundary of Beverley Close (also the perimeter of Hartleton Farm) is also identifiable as a low bank (**32**) along the bracken/tree line on the south east corner of this open greensward.

3. KINGSTON's boundary with Ham changed substantially several times over the centuries and in 1994 the small remaining part was included within the Borough of Richmond.

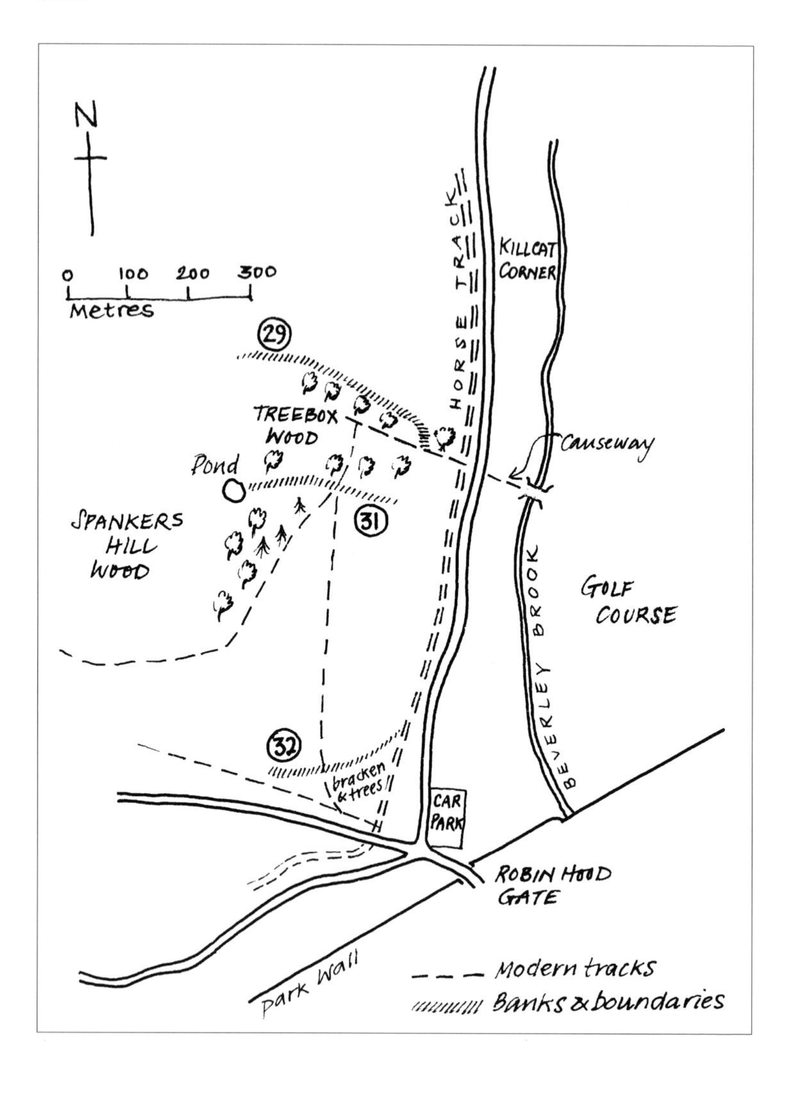
N
0 100 200 300
Metres
29
TREEBOX WOOD
Pond
31
SPANKERS HILL WOOD
HORSE TRACK
KILLCAT CORNER
Causeway
BEVERLEY BROOK
GOLF COURSE
32
bracken & trees
CAR PARK
ROBIN HOOD GATE
Park Wall
Modern tracks
Banks & boundaries

4. The PETERSHAM-HAM boundary is almost impossible to follow, except approximately. But a large ivy clad ancient oak standing by the pond in the south-east corner of the Sudbrook golf course (part of the original park) may be one of the old boundary oaks that ran almost straight up the escarpment and across to southern corner of the White Ash Lodge boundary fence, and then just a few paces west of the northern tip of the Upper Pen Pond.

5. Part of Beverley Brook was once a boundary between Mortlake and Ham on one bank and Wimbledon with its sub-manors of Roehampton and Putney on the other.

The Isabella Plantation

Leave your car at the Broomfield Hill Car park.

INTRODUCTION

The final walk – especially if some of the longer walks proved a bit of a slog – is a well-earned leisurely stroll, ideal after a heavy Sunday lunch. There is neither a prescribed route nor a particular season for this woodland garden. It is most popular in April-May when the camellias, azaleas and rhododendrons are in bloom. But the show of colour can distract from the more satisfying quality of the garden, the interplay of shape, light and shade. Be guided by the map (p.150) and go where you will. Most of the delights, as in the rest of the park, are those of personal discovery. A brief history follows for those whose appetite for history remains undiminished, followed by the main garden features, a sketch map and a monthly listing of what to look out for.

A BRIEF HISTORY

The Isabella Slade was originally planted by Lord Sidmouth in 1831, with subsequent additions, first on the north east side in 1845, and then an enlargement of virtually the whole outer edge of the plantation in 1865. This planting was superimposed on some of the pre-enclosure oak pollards of Black Heath (on Lane's map, p.66).

How it came by the name Isabella is unclear. It is possible it was named after the wife or daughter of a member of staff but the name is at least 200 years old, appearing as 'Isabella Slade' on a map dated 1771. Lane's map shows the area was called The Sleyt (a sheep walk) in the early seventeenth century. Isabella may well be a corruption of 'isabel', which once meant a dingy or greyish yellow and would have referred to the colour of the sandy clay topsoil. The word has an unsavoury origin. In 1601 the Archduchess Isabella of Austria, Infanta of Spain and Governor of the Spanish Netherlands, vowed not to change her linen until Ostend had been recaptured from the Protestant Dutch. Never *ever* make a vow in the heat of the moment. The siege lasted for three years (1601-1604) and her counsellors must have faced the routine noxious ordeal of advising their unnecessarily malodorous governor. The name Isabel became a byword for grubby discolouration.

Prior to the development of Isabella Plantation in 1950, there was just a small pool (Still Pond) fed by a spring, and a muddy wallow at the foot of the slope in open parkland (now Peg's Pond). Both ponds, dug in 1861, were for the watering of livestock.

The present woodland walk is largely the inspiration of Wally Miller, head gardener and George Thomson, park superintendent, 1951-71, the former now immortalised with Wally's Island in Peg's Pond, and the latter with Thomson's Pond in the centre of the plantation and also with the wooden stumps that line the carriageways of the park, known as 'Thomson's teeth'. This is a classic twentieth century garden concept, something that certainly would not now be allowed inside Richmond Park with its present emphasis on preservation of the natural ecology, deprecating the introduction of exotics, like rhododendron species. Thomson cleared the *Rhododendron ponticum* which is

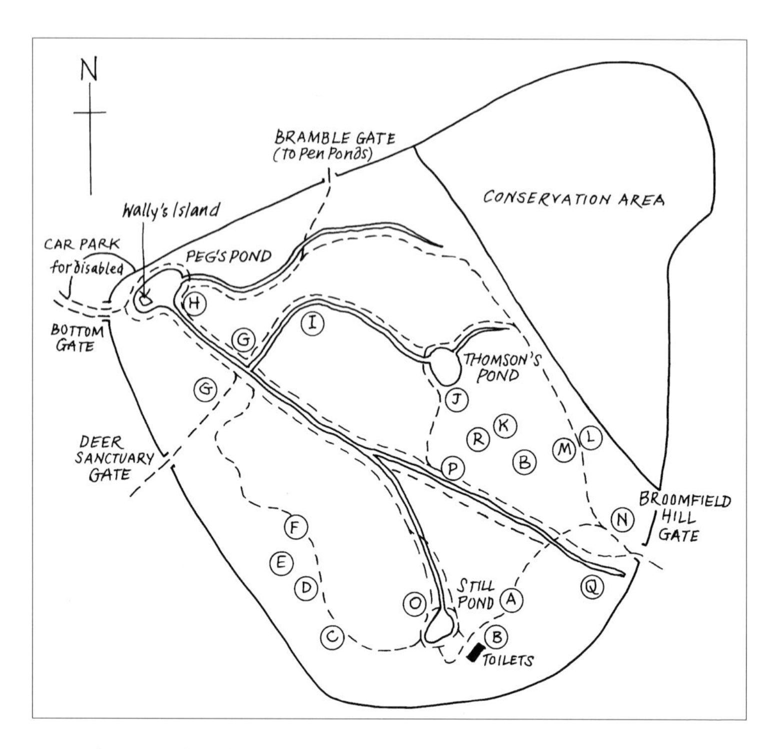

so widespread in the park but kept it here as a framework for this woodland garden. He planted other rhododendron species and also Kurume Azaleas around Still Pond.

The Main Stream running from Broomfield Gate was dug in 1960, the water initially pumped from the Sidmouth Plantation reservoir (visible behind the section of feather-edged wooden fence from Pembroke Lodge car park), and the Plantation enlarged to incorporate Peg's Pond. Since 1976 the water has been pumped from the Pen Ponds to feed each stream. A third stream was dug in the early 1980s through the wilder northern section, where the stream banks have been colonized by ferns, water plantains and brook lime.

THE MAIN FEATURES

The Heather Garden (G) was created in the open area outside the tree canopy. Some species of heather are in flower virtually all the year round.

Still Pond acts as a dark mirror reflecting the azalea and rhododendron blooms in spring, and the *Acer palmatum* (Japanese maple) foliage in autumn. It is also edged with *Iris sibirica*.

Thomson's Pond is edged with purple loosestrife, sedge, iris and contains water lilies.

Peg's Pond contains tougher plants (the diving ducks wiped out the water lilies): flag iris, willow herb, sedge, water forget-me-nots. **The Bog Garden (I)** is currently composed of rush, molinia and other grasses, bamboo, pontaderia, a grove *of Gunnera manicata* (with enormous foliage) and *Osmunda regalis* (large ferns).

Acer Glade (M) is planted with nine different species of maple that provide spectacular autumn foliage and boast highly characteristic bark.

Wilson's Glade (N), named after Ernest Wilson, the plant collector (see under *Azaleas* below), immediately to the right of Broomfield Hill Gate has already been planted with trees and bulbs, mainly introductions he himself made.

The pre-enclosure oak pollards (D) west of Still Pond are worth examining for their calloused hollow trunks, and the beef steak fungi that grow in them particularly in autumn.

Multi-stemmed beeches grow in several parts of the garden. Their curious growth is something of an enigma.

The oak that grows in the embrace of a beech (O) is another curiosity to be found near the north-west side of Still Pond.

THE FLORA

The garden is full of both common and rare plant species. Here are a few basic notes about some of the more notable species present.

Azaleas The garden contains 15 known varieties of deciduous azalea. In addition the national collection of Kurume Azaleas (the 'Wilson 50') was started in the garden in 1991. These are the 50 evergreen azalea species assembled and made available in the West from 1919 onwards by the British plant collector Ernest Wilson, from 250 named kinds cultivated at the time in Kurume, Japan. (Incidentally, there is a local connection, for Coombe Wood, just outside Ladderstile Gate, was the nursery of James Veitch who first commissioned Wilson to collect plants for him in China.)

Rhododendrons There are 50 different species of rhododendron and 120 hybrids in the Plantation.

BIRD LIFE

It is sometimes forgotten that the good ground and tree cover makes the Isabella Plantation ideal for small animals, particularly birds.

Residents include redpolls, chaffinches, bullfinches, greenfinches, goldcrests, treecreepers, nuthatches, blue tits, coal tits, great tits, long tailed tits, dunnocks, lesser and greater spotted woodpeckers, as well as blackbirds, song thrushes, sparrow hawks and tawny owls. Waterfowl include plain and red crested pochards, tuffed ducks, shelducks, pintails, moorhens, coots.

Visitors include perennials like the herons and other park residents and also

(i) Spring: garden and wood warblers, redstarts, cuckoos, common and lesser whitethroats.
(ii) Summer: blackcaps, spotted flycatchers.
(iii) Autumn: many of the above visitors, and also green sandpipers.
(iv) Winter: siskins, kingfishers, reed buntings.

Butterflies in the Plantation include: Commas, Small Tortoiseshells, Wall Browns, Red Admirals, Peacocks, Meadow Browns, Speckled Woods, Small Heaths, Small Coppers, Purple Hairstreaks, Brimstones, Small and Large Skippers, Common Blues.

Dragonflies include Emperor dragonflies, Broad-bodied Chasers, Brown Hawkers, Common Darters and Golden Ringed dragonflies.

Damselflies include blue-tailed, common blue and small red varieties.

WHAT TO LOOK OUT FOR EACH MONTH

January

- By Broomfield Hill Gate (on right side of path) the Chinese Witch Hazel with fragrant yellow tassled flowers.
- Set back south of Acer Glade the Chinese *Mahonia bealei* displaying yellow flowers with lily of the valley fragrance and *Viburnum tinus* (the Laurustinus) an evergreen shrub with white flowers; and also *Rhododendron dauricum* 'Midwinter' in rose-purple flower by Acer Glade path.
- At Peg's Pond the pollarded willow *(Salix alba)* with red and amber stems.

- On the north side of the Main Stream **(P)** two river birches *(Betula nigra)* one above the Heather Garden and the other nearer Broomfield Hill Gate.
- Set back below Camellia Walk **(A)**, Camellia 'J.C. Williams' with single pink flowers.

February

- On Camellia Walk **(A)** early Camellias include 'J.C. Williams 'Mary Christian' and 'Wabisuke'.
- On the wet lawn **(Q)** near Broomfield Hill Gate early dwarf *Narcissus cyclamineus* with its long yellow trumpets and swept back petals.
- Below Still Pond *Rhododendron shilsonii* with deep red flowers. Other rhododendrons on the Main Stream, set back from Camellia Walk.

March

- Camellia Walk, several varieties in bloom.
- Set back in woodland west of Still Pond, *Magnolia campbellii* ssp. *mollicomata* **(F)**, huge rose pink flowers.
- Above the Heather Garden on the Main Stream, *Pieris floribunda,* an evergreen shrub with drooping pitcher-shaped white flowers.
- Halfway up the Main Stream, opposite Thomson's Pond, *Rhododendron lanigerum* with vivid red flowers.

April

- Along the streams marsh marigolds *(Caltha palustris)* and American Skunk Cabbage *(Lysichiton americanum)* with its yellow hooded spathes.
- Halfway up the Main Stream *Rhodendendron 'Emasculum',* thus named because the flowers lack stamens. Despite this apparently tragic deficiency, they make a nice rose-

lilac mound of blossom. Further upstream *Rhododendron augustinii,* a blue-flowered species from China, and its hybrid form, *'Electra'*.

May

This is the month that most of the azaleas, rhododendrons and magnolias let rip. Apart from the display around Still Pond, the two beds of dwarf rhododendrons, *Rhododendron yakushimanum,* surrounded by its hybrids named after 'The Seven Dwarfs' **(K)** are worth seeing on the lawn south of Thomson's Pond. Look out, too, for the Dove-tree **(B)**, the flowers of which resemble hanging handkerchiefs, hence its other name: 'Handkerchief-tree'. There is one south of Thomson's Pond which has just started flowering, and another on the eastern path from Camellia Walk to the toilets which is mature enough to flower any year now.

June

Apart from late flowering rhodondendrons and azaleas, look out for:

- Along the streams, *Primula japonica,* in red, white and magenta forms, and also the Iris family: *ensate, sibirica,* and *pseudoacorus* (the native yellow flag iris).
- Just above the confluence of the Main Stream and that from Thomson's Pond, *Stewartia pseudocamellia,* white camellia-like flowers, flaking bark.
- Just above Still Pond the Snow-bell tree *(Styrax japonica)* with small bell-shaped flowers.
- About 50 yards west of Still Pond, near the beginning of Beech Walk, a *Magnolia sinensis* **(C)** in bloom.

July

- In the south west corner of the Plantation, near Still Pond and Camellia Walk, late flowering rhododendrons.

- Halfway down Beech Walk, 'Swamp Honesuckle' *(Rhododendron viscosum)* with a spicy fragrance.
- Thomson's and Peg's ponds are by now both frantic with dragonflies. Also on Thomson's pond Pickerel Weed's blue flower spikes and tall spear shaped leaves.
- Along the streams varieties of the 'Day Lily' *(Hemerocallis)* in flower among the irises.

August

- On the lawn south of Thomson's Pond *Magnolia grandiflora*.
- At the southern end of Acer Glade a sweet pepper bush *(Clethra)* with fragrant bell-shaped cream flowers.
- Along the streams native marginal plants, purple and yellow loosestrife, meadowsweet and greater willow herb.

September

- Near the wild stream through the north of the garden, *Hydrangea quercifolia* has papery panicles deepening into pink, and rough oak shaped leaves with bronze autumnal tints.
- Above Thomson's Pond, *Sorbus sargentiana* bears heads of small berries ripening to reddish-orange with red foliage, and nearby groups of the Guelder Rose *(Viburnum opulus)* with glossy red berries.
- A short walk down the main path from Broomfield Hill Gate, an unidentified magnolia bears large ovoid fruits like pineapples covered in curved spines.

October

- Near Thomson's pond, two Tupelo trees turning brilliant scarlet; a group of shrubs 'Persian Ironwood' *(Parrotia persica)* amber, crimson and gold foliage.
- Close to Broomfield Gate, *Fothergilla monticola* with variegated fiery red and yellow foliage.

- Acers throughout the garden assume autumn tints.
- Above Still Pond the *Acer palmatum* assumes red foliage. A young tulip tree may be found on Thomson's Lawn, its foliage now turning butter yellow.

November

- On the edge of Thomson's Pond, the Strawberry Tree **(J)** bears waxy bell-shaped pink flowers.
- Near the confluence of Still Pond Stream and Main Stream, *Camellia sasanqua 'Rubra'*, with small single fragrant flowers.
- By Peg's Pond the Swamp cypress *(Taxodium distichum)* **(H)** foliage goes bronze in autumn.
- *Osmunda regalis,* the Royal Fern forms rusty clumps beside streams and ponds.
- *Viburnum betulifolium* in Wilson's Glade, characterised by red berries.

December

- By Broomfield Hill Gate, *Viburnum x bodnantese* shrub with fragrant pink flowers.
- By Peg's pond, pollarded willows with red and amber stems, and *Cornus stolonifera* with yellow/green stems under the nearby weeping willow tree.
- Above Thomson's Pond young birches with white stems, and east of the Pond *Prunus serrula,* mahogany red bark peeling in curly shreds.
- Throughout the garden snake-bark acers. Look out for the 'Stinking Hellebore' with its green flowers in the wilder parts of the garden.

How do we want our park?

It is easy to think that Richmond Park jogs along happily enough through the seasons, with nature doing its stuff and the light touch of its custodians keeping everything within reasonable bounds. Such a roseate view is untruthful to the reality. The Royal Parks staff are continually faced with invidious choices, fundamentally between using the park as a public amenity and treating it as a wildlife preserve.

Getting the balance right is extraordinarily difficult, partly because of the pressure of lobby groups but also because it is so difficult to measure what is really going on over a short time span. Unless one has a sharp eye for detail, there seems to be a stable *status quo*. In reality no such *status quo* exists. You need not be an ecologist to recognise that the scene, despite the Royal Parks' best efforts over the years, is one of slow but progressive diminishment of the wild life. This becomes apparent when one applies measurements over a longer time span. Take bird life, for example. In 1894 one walker reported that nightingales were so plentiful in Sidmouth Wood 'that it might well be called Nightingale Grove'. Nightingales love thickets and coppice. Perhaps the park no longer has enough of these. Nightingales get noticed at night when their first soft '*pew, pew,*' begins to rise to their impassioned crescendo, pouring forth their souls abroad in ecstasy, as Keats so famously put it. They still frequented all the major woods and plantations in the first decades of the twentieth century, but then declined rapidly and ceased to inhabit the park from about 1930.

Here is another tale of loss. Nightjars were common here in 1900. The park's open grassland and bracken were their perfect habitat. They would lie up in the grass during the daytime, taking flight to hunt at night. The hen would incubate her eggs on the ground. But the last pair to have produced young in the park was probably in the 1930s, barely within living memory. Grey partridge were still common in Richmond Park in the 1930s, when coveys of ten or more birds were not unusual. In 1938, however, the superintendent reported that partridges 'have a very rough time, during the breeding season, from dogs, etc.', and by the 1980s partridge were a rare sight indeed. Today any partridge seen are almost certainly escapees from elsewhere. Skylarks, the next, it seems, on this fell list, were numerous throughout the twentieth century but now require protection to encourage them to breed in the park.

Consider mammals. It is reckoned that the park has lost some 40 per cent of its mammal species during the twentieth century. The most obvious recent loss is the hare. The hare is among the most mystical beasts of the field, associated with magic, witchcraft and trickery. It is embedded deeply in our folk-memory, probably predating a literate society. Forget about Easter bunnies. The true pre-Christian symbol of Easter was not the rabbit but the hare, which 'laid' the Easter eggs that children across the centuries have enjoyed and wondered at. It is, appropriately for Easter, the potent symbol of the spring, of regeneration and of new life. A late thirteenth century English poem gives the hare many names, among them 'the way-beater', 'the hedge-frisker', 'the stag-of-the-stubble', 'the light-foot', 'the sitter-still', and 'the one who goes not straight home'.

We had all this poetry, not just in words but in the wonderful living creature itself, until we banished it.

Because it lives in the grass the hare must be the beast of ultimate cunning and so it is, outwitting its pursuers. Two decades before Richmond Park was enclosed, a naturalist wrote of the doe, or 'fennel' as the suckling female was known in Surrey:

> 'She keepeth not her young ones together in one litter, but layeth them a furlong from one another, that so she may not lose them altogether, if peradventure men or beasts light upon them.'

So hares need space. In 1938 the park superintendent saw seven hares together one morning. How much would you give for such a sight today? But he had already introduced regulations to protect them against greyhounds. He was well aware of the dangers noting, 'They are extremely graceful and pretty animals, and it would be a very great pity to see them ousted from Richmond Park entirely'. But ousted they eventually were, though they were still common in the 1950s. Yet even their cunning could not stave off the catastrophe wrought by the sheer weight of human intrusion in the 1960s. The last hare was recorded in 1972. Lament our banishment of the light-foot, the hedge-frisker, the way-beater. One might speculate about other smaller mammals and dread what may have happened to them. Stoats were numerous in 1906 and there may be a few around, but the last recorded sighting was in 1935. As elsewhere, red squirrels were ousted by the grey following the latter's deliberate introduction early in the twentieth century. What about reptiles? Grass snakes are very occasionally spotted. When was an adder last found? There seems to be no record and it is unlikely any are left, yet the old name Adder Down testifies to their presence here once.

We can also look at the terrain. In the mid-nineteenth century Josiah Parkes drained almost all the boggy areas of the park, making it much drier to walk across but at the expense of the natural ecology. In the early twentieth century two attempts were made to straighten Beverley Brook, thus losing the sluggish and marshy areas that had made it a rich natural environment. In the seventeenth century the stream had been noted for its brown trout. In the interests of greater efficiency, parts of the bank were also concreted in 1930-37, thus rendering life impossible for the few water voles that had been here. Too late for them, the concrete has now been broken out. With the closure of Worcester Park Sewage Works in the 1990s, the brook no longer receives raw sewage and this marks the beginning of a slow but limited recovery, in small fish and in kingfishers. There are plans to reintroduce water vole into feeder streams, the brook itself being no longer suitable for the vole.

From the late nineteenth century we have, in the natural world, acted like bulls in a china shop:

O if we but knew what we do
When we delve or hew –
Hack and rack the growing green!
Since our country is so tender
To touch, her being so slender,
That, like this sleek and seeing ball
But a prick will make no eye at all,
Where we, even where we mean
To mend her we end her,
When we hew or delve.

G.M. Hopkins, *Binsey Poplars* (felled 1879)

At its best, humankind enjoys a symbiotic relationship with the land, but Gerard Manley Hopkins was surely right to plead for preservation of the weeds and the wilderness. In managing (alas, so controlling a word) the landscape we must be informed with the eye of understanding and love. To its credit, the Royal Parks has started to allow old land drains to silt up naturally, to encourage recovery of the wildness and wet, but there is still a long way to go.

If we ask why the foregoing animal species abandoned this incomparable stretch of London grassland, we know the only truthful answer: excessive human activity. This activity comes in various forms: too many walkers, too many dogs and too many cars. In 1944 the superintendent reported a great and unanticipated result of war: 'the Park, as a whole, now so free of dogs, people, horses and cars, has become a sanctuary at large.' The war bought the Park about ten years' grace before it came under greater pressure. We walkers trample. Were there fewer of us it would not matter but now that we trample the park in such large numbers we need to think about the implications and walk with greater awareness and care.

If it is not we ourselves, then it is our dogs. Fifteen years ago there were just over 1,000 dogs coming into the park each day and the number must have increased since then. It has been estimated that these dogs deposit at least 100 tons of excrement in the park each year. If that seems a lot, it is apparently a severely conservative estimate. Does excrement just rot down innocently into the soil? It does not. Dog fouling unnaturally enriches the soil, changing the flora where there has been contamination. It leaves an excess of phosphates and nitrogen in the soil. The evidence is visible from the air, where photography shows a 'halo' of more intense green around car parks, where dogs pee. The flora has been changed. This is no urban myth but the subject of scientific monitoring. More obviously ominous, the medication given to dogs makes its way into the soil, where it harms invertebrates and possibly other creatures. Following the annual cull each year the venison may not be sold as organic because of the chemicals that may have been ingested by the deer when feeding on polluted grass. What, then, may we imagine is happening to the small mammals or the reptiles, invertebrates and insects? In allowing dogs to defecate we cannot be doing any favours to the park as a wildlife habitat.

Crows, which were a rarity in 1900, feed upon the dog faeces, upon bread, etc., brought in for the waterfowl and upon other litter left in the park. In fact crows greatly depend upon human activity. When the park was closed for a mere six weeks in early 2001, on account of Foot and Mouth Disease, crow numbers fell dramatically. The great number of crows is yet another major menace for small birds, particularly for those that incubate their eggs on the ground.

Acid grassland is an acknowledged priority habitat for conservation in Britain because of the special flora and fauna. Here we have the largest and most important acid grassland in the Greater London area. It is an important and endangered habitat but one might not guess it. In allowing dogs to run off the leash we have rendered these grasslands too stressful for hares and ground nesting birds. The deer sanctuary in High Wood was abandoned a couple of years ago because dogs ran through the area thus rendering the sanctuary pointless.

And if it is not our dogs, it is our cars. Until the closure of Robin Hood Gate in 2003, approximately 3,700 cars crossed the park per hour during peak periods, spewing forth car emissions – a cocktail of pollutants including various forms of nitrogen, carbon, ammonia, particulates and metals – which adversely affect the acid grasslands and probably the mammals, reptiles and invertebrates which live on them. Monitoring revealed that the park was carrying a traffic load equivalent to an urban dual carriageway in rush hour. This gate closure has achieved a 12 per cent or so overall reduction in traffic. Yet we know, because it is true everywhere else, that the traffic flow will slowly build up again over the next few years.

We need to think about what the traffic does to the park. At its crudest, the long processions of cars and the noise they create diminish the quality of the park for walkers. Yet that is scarcely as important as the environmental issue. The adverse affect of pollutants is easily measurable up to 200 metres on open grassland and 100 metres in oakwood. Nutrient enrichment, principally forms of nitrogen and ammonia, certainly distort flora and probably affect the fauna. Metals (wear and tear), which affect soil chemistry, are traceable up to 30 metres away from the roadside: the bigger the car, the greater the damage. One effect for nearby trees is increased leaf temperature and even abrasion of leaf surfaces. The trees may not die but their health is diminished.

Then there is the noise of the traffic. We know that high levels of urban noise increase stress levels among humans. Precisely the same is true for birds and probably for other mammals. Dutch studies show a substantial reduction in bird density and also their capacity to breed even 2km from a highway. Slower traffic speeds in the park undoubtedly ameliorate this but when we know that there is a very high loss in breeding capacity close to busy roads we should treat the danger seriously. Birdsong, essential for breeding, must rise above traffic noise or must be modified to beat the human-altered environment. Not every bird species can manage this. So we lose some.

We urgently need strategies to reduce our impact upon the park in all three respects and to find ways in which we can both enjoy the park but limit our behaviour sufficiently to reduce the stress which inhibits the wildlife. If we can achieve this we shall enrich not only the park but also ourselves.

In Ancient Egypt the hieroglyph signifying the verb 'to exist' was a ripple of water and above it an animal, the hare.

It was closely associated with the idea of Creation. The message from Ancient Egypt crosses the millennia as a sharp rebuke to our reckless desecration of nature. The twentieth century tale of progressive diminishment in Richmond Park was not inevitable. It has been the result of thoughtlessness, ignorance and a deep-seated reluctance to heed warnings. We did not, for example, listen when previous superintendents warned of the dangers of diminishment through human activity. Nor did we heed the warnings of those who pleaded in the early 1960s to protect the park from through-traffic.

The process of diminishment need not be irreversible. Richmond Park has been designated

- a Grade 1 Heritage Site,
- a National Nature Reserve,
- a Site of Special Scientific Interest,
- a European Area of Special Conservation and, more parochially,
- a Site of Metropolitan Importance to Nature Conservation.

Such designations almost beggar belief when one considers the substantial decline in habitat in this great park over the twentieth century. Do they now mean this decline will be reversed? A successful reversal is far from assured.

The Royal Parks does what it can but it struggles against powerful lobbies. We cannot ask it to save the day without a strong constituency of informed public support in favour of progressive wild life enhancement and of a measured and relatively modest rolling back of the tidal weight of human activity. A revival of this kind can only be achieved first by a conscious acknowledgement that the diminishment is the result of public fecklessness and then by co-operating in strategies to achieve the necessary levels of self-restraint in the way we use the park. We have a London Wetlands Centre in Barnes. We marvel at it and do not question the restrictions placed upon us there. If Richmond Park were formally designated as 'London's Grasslands' this need not lead to anything like the strictly observed rules necessary in Barnes, but it could lead to stronger guidelines and restraints on our activities, ones which, even if we found them inconvenient, would help educate us about what we so easily destroy. We must learn progressively to curb our level of activity if we want to see any return at all of the creatures which once enriched human delight here. The process may be too slow for us to enjoy the rewards in our own lifetime, but we owe it to our children and their children to shift the balance back in favour of Nature Restored.

APPENDIX 1

The principal plants of Richmond Park

The following pages attempt to provide a very basic guide to some of the more notable flora in the park. Regrettably there is insufficient room to provide sketches of the variety of grasses, let alone the wild flowers. If you are that interested, you need a pocket guide. Wild flower manuals are easily obtainable. Those who wish to find out about grasses can hardly do better than find an old copy of C.E Hubbard's *Grasses* (Pelican, 1959), or the Collins Pocket Guide, *Grasses, Sedges, Rushes and Ferns* (by Richard and Alastair Fitter).

The following is not intended to be exhaustive but to provide brief notes on flora that struck me as of general interest, almost certainly too detailed for some and too brief for others. It is laid out in the following order:

1. Trees
2. Shrubs
3. Acidic and upland grasses & rushes
4. Other acid grassland plants
5. Coarser grasses, etc.

1. PRINCIPAL TREES

Alder (*Alnus glutinosa*) Alders grow where their roots will be wet. 'Alder Hill' on the enclosure map indicates that there were probably alders growing along the stream that now takes water from the Pen Ponds to Beverley Brook.

Ash, Common (*Fraxinus excelsior*) The largest specimens are in the Isabella Plantation. The name Ashen Close on the enclosure map (see p.65) indicates that ashes were growing here 400 years ago, presumably as a feature of the hedgerows. The Shrew Ash grew on the southern boundary bank of Ashen Close until its final decayed remnants were destroyed in the storm of 1987. Reverence for the magical qualities of ash trees is recorded from early times in Britain and northern Europe, and these were often deliberately cloven. In his *Natural History of Selborne,* Gilbert White gives an account of the supposed medicinal properties of the ash. The Shrew Ash derives its name from the insertion of a live shrew into a hole bored into the trunk, which was then stopped up, as an antidote to sickness. The tree was still resorted to in the mid-

The Shrew Ash before its partial destruction in 1875. Note the bar over which the sick child was passed. The woman may be a 'shrew mother'.

nineteenth century as a source of healing for sick children and animals. A child was apparently cured by being passed nine times around a wooden bar wedged in the cleavage of the tree. This feat could only be performed by a 'shrew mother', a woman versed in the ritual doggerel of the healing process. Sir Richard Owen observed several groups visit the tree before its partial destruction in 1875.

Beech, Common (*Fagus sylvatica*) Prefers chalk or well-drained sands. There are only about 70 mature beech trees in the park. Beeches were deliberately planted in the eighteenth and nineteenth centuries as trees that ornamented the landscape. The Beech Walk running northwards from Pembroke Lodge towards Richmond Gate has now nearly disappeared. Relatively young beeches line the old medieval track running up from Ham Cross to Dann's Pond. There are some fine beeches at the top of Broomfield Hill, clearly intended to enhance the view.

Birch The silver birch (*Betula pendula*) is native to light soils and gravels, a characteristic tree on heaths. Apart from the Silver Jubilee clump planted on the site of the old bandstand near Richmond Gate in 1977, they proliferate in Sidmouth Wood, Isabella and Pond Plantations. Birch, an early coloniser, usually lives for less than 100 years, by which time other tree species deny the light needed for its regeneration. Its airborne seed finds fresh open spaces to colonise.

Chestnut The sweet chestnut (*Castanea sativa*) was probably introduced to Britain by the Romans. How long it has been in the park is impossible to say. It was certainly planted in the nineteenth century to provide autumn deer feed. Some trees may well have been planted earlier. A few still mark the avenue leading away from King Henry VIII's Mound, depicted on the

Kip engraving of 1708, but it is unclear whether the trees he illustrated were Sweet Chestnuts or another species.

Hawthorn The common or hedgerow hawthorn (*Crataegus monogyna*) is a native to this landscape. It was here as a hedgerow plant before the park enclosure. Its name describes it perfectly, for *haw* or *haga* meant hedge, fence or enclosure in Anglo-Saxon. On the enclosure map, all the closes and many of the fields would have been hedged with hawthorn and gorse, between which other interlopers would seed. Twenty per cent of the veteran hawthorns in the Park are reckoned to be woodland (or Midland) hawthorn (*Crataegus laevigata*). In the middle ages this was more common than the common hawthorn, until the conscious propagation of the latter for hedging purposes reversed this pattern. The woodland hawthorn is distinguished by rounded shallow lobed leaves and, when in flower, by two styles leading to two pips. Its importance when reading the landscape is as an indicator of undisturbed land that must once, if no longer, have been woodland.

Horse Chestnut (*Aesculus hippocastanum*) This tree was planted in the nineteenth and twentieth centuries when it became a popular plant for public spaces. It is an exotic, having been introduced to Britain from Illyria/Albania in the early seventeenth century. It was probably planted to provide supplementary autumn feed for the deer herds. It is unrelated to the sweet chestnut.

Lime (*Tilia x europaea*) The common lime was deliberately planted in the park in the nineteenth century, notably along the park fringes. It is a hybrid between two native species: the large and small leafed limes. It became a popular tree for public places, particularly for avenues, on account of its compact shape.

Maple (field maple) (*Acer campestre*) A native which was growing here naturally before the enclosure, particularly in hedgerows. A fine veteran specimen may be found in the narrow neck of grassland between Prince Charles' Spinney and the Isabella Plantation (Tree No.1384). One hundred **sugar maples** (*Acer saccharum*), planted by Gallows Pond near Kingston Gate, were a gift of the Government of Ontario in 1969, marking the centenary of Ontario's first official representation in the United Kingdom.

Oak The common, **English, or pedunculate oak** (*Quercus robur)* dominates the tree landscape in the park. Of over 3,000 oaks in the park, about 450 oaks date back to pre-enclosure times are all pedunculate. Some of these are over 600 years old. The pedunculate is the predominant native oak of the east and south of Britain, since it prefers the prevailing heavy soils of the lowlands. A small number of **sessile or durmast oak**, (*Quercus petraea*) have been planted since 1800. The sessile oak predominates naturally in north and western Britain, since it prefers lighter, more acid soils. But both varieties will willingly grow outside their preferred region. When in leaf they are easy to differentiate. The pedunculate bears its acorns on long stalks (hence its name), while its leaves grow almost straight off the stem, with 'ears' or auricles close to the join

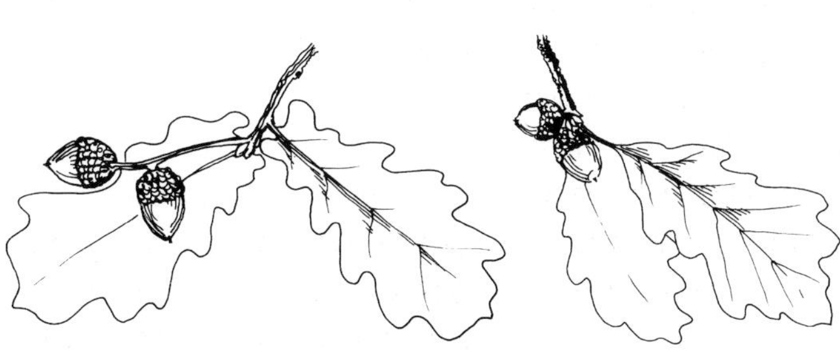

with the stem. The Sessile is the opposite, acorns growing straight off the stem, while the leaves are without auricles and grow on stalks. But one must beware hybrids between the two. The pollarding of oaks is discussed on p.23. There are two familiar natural characteristics of the oak. In maturity it begins to die back, abandoning some of its furthest branches, while lower branches spread out. Such trees are 'stag-headed' or, in Surrey *patois*, 'sproddy'. The other characteristic, most notably in the pedunculate, is the zig-zag habit of its branches, so useful to medieval carpenters. This habit is due to the persistent growth of single lateral buds off the parent branch, while the terminal bud that might continue the straight progress of the parent branch tends to die.

Red oak (*Quercus rubra*) is an exotic, introduced to Britain from eastern Canada and the United States in 1724. It was planted in clumps probably some time between 1850 and 1920.

Turkey oak (*Quercus cerris*) is an exotic, native of southern Europe and introduced to Britain in 1735 because of its vigorous growth for timber production.

Sycamore The sycamore (*Acer pseudoplatanus*) is a member of the maple family, possibly introduced by the Romans and certainly here since the fourteenth century, but a native of central and southern Europe. Its fecundity and invasive propensity can excite startlingly antagonistic reactions. Yet while it hosts a small variety of animal species, it boasts significantly more aphid life than most trees, thus providing an important food resource for small birds. Furthermore, its grain produces a veneer like watered silk. So here is a fact to stop you in your tracks: a large sycamore, sold in the 1960s for over £1,000, contained sufficient veneer to cover five football pitches.

Willow (crack willow) (*Salix fragilis*) Native to Britain and almost certainly a native to the park where it may be found in several wet areas. Its habit of snapping off leads to its branches rooting themselves in the ground. This is a principal means of regeneration. It was deliberately planted along the canalised part of the Beverley Brook in the 1930s, and is routinely pollarded so, if you wish to, you can see this form of tree surgery in action.

TREE PLANTATIONS

Many of the plantations listed below were clearly superimposed on previously wooded areas. Barn Wood and High Wood, to name but two, have some medieval trees extant; Duchess and Sawpit woods were also medieval but thickened later. We also know from maps that Richmond - Sheen and Sheen - Roehampton belts and trees along the Thatched House Lodge portion of the escarpment existed before 1771, but may have begun to suffer depletion.

Dates of tree plantings: (As you walk you may like to refer to the vintage of any woods you pass through)

Barn Wood .... medieval
Beech Walk c.1840
Beverley Brook 1838
Broomfield Hill Plantations, ... West 1880, East 1878
Conduit Wood 1829
Coronation Plantation (SE of Thatched House Lodge) 1902
Coronation Plantation (NE of Thatched House Lodge) 1953
Duchess Wood .... eighteenth cent., possibly pre-enclosure
George Vth Jubilee Plantation 1935
Gibbet Wood 1878
Golf course-Roehampton belt 1936

Ham Belt.. 1825-29
High Wood.. medieval
Hornbeam Walk.. c. 1834
Isabella Plantation .... core 1831, 1845, edges 1865
Jubilee Plantation.. 1887
Kidney Wood 1829
Killcat Corner 1864
King Clump (nr. Kingston Gate)..................................... 1901
Kingston Hill Plantation (along wall)............................. 1826
Lawn Plantation 1883
Lower Pen Pond 1903
Pond Plantation ....East 1824, West 1865
Prince Charles' Spinney 1951
Richmond Gate Woods... 1850
Queen Elizabeth Wood... 1948
Queen Mother's Copse (NE of White Lodge).......................... 1980
Roehampton Plantation (to Sheen) 1825
Sheen Cross Wood.. 1819
Sawpit Plantation...................................West 1873, East 1874
Sidmouth Wood ....North-east 1823, South-west 1830
Spanker's Hill Wood,...............................East 1819, West 1824
Star and Garter Hill pre-1850
Teck Plantation 1905
Tercentenary Plantation 1937
Treebox Wood (NE of Spankers Hill) 1877
Two Storm Wood... 1991
Victory Plantation.. 1946
White Lodge Wood ....North 1873, South 1879

2. SHRUBS

Bracken (*Pteridium aquilinum*), barely a shrub, is associated with sandy drift soils overlaying the clay.

Gorse (*Ulex europaeus*) is a classic native acid land shrub. The seedlings and shoots are soft and highly nutritious to grazers. It therefore needs some protection from the deer herds. It provides important shelter for wildlife.

Heather (*Calluna vulgaris*) **or ling** must have been widespread here once. One tiny patch in the grassland between Pond and Isabella Plantations has survived, a remnant of the heath that must have been here.

Rhododendron (*Rhododendron ponticum*) was planted in several parts of the park in the nineteenth century, doubtless to give 'colour', notably in Sidmouth Wood, Upper Pen Pond Plantation and on Spanker's Hill, quite apart from the Isabella Plantation. It is a native of the northern parts of Asia Minor. It is one of the four or five principal invasive exotic species that is difficult to eradicate and threatens the landscape.

3. ACIDIC AND UPLAND GRASSES AND RUSHES

Drier upland areas have fine grasses, mostly bents and fescues. Here are some of the more common of these grasses: **common bent** (*Agrostis tenuis*); **sweet vernal grass** (*Anthoxanthum odoratum*) an early herald of summer with long panicles of bright stamens; **red fescue** (*Festuca rubra*); **wavy hair grass** (*Deschampsia flexuosa*). **Mat grass** (*Nardus stricta*) is a London scarcity. It has dense matted tufts with hard bristle-like leaves, in the despairing words of one manual: 'Grass lovers are at a loss to find recommendations for it.'

Look out for **early hair-grass** (*Aira praecox L.*). It is densely tufted, seldom reaches more than 8cm in height and colonises anthills.

Wetter areas (principal location Pond Slade) have some grasses but also sedges and rushes: **Brown or velvet bent** (*Agrostis canina*); tussock grasses such as **tufted hair grass** (*Deschampsia cespitosa*); **purple moor grass** (*Molinia caerulea*); Rushes: **common rush** (*Juncus conglomeratus*); **sharp flowered rus**h (*Juncus acutiflorus*); **soft rush** (*Juncus effusus*); **common spike Rush** (*Eleocharis palustris*). **Common reeds** (*Phragmites australis*) will be found around the southern end of the Upper Pen Pond.

Acid grassland wildflower species in the park are numerous. Here is a small sample:

Lady's smock (*Cardamine pratensis*), known also as **Milkmaids** but in Surrey as **smell-smock**, it inhabits wet ground.

Tormentil *(Potentilla erecta)* has delicate small yellow flowers

Bird's foot trefoil (*Lotus corniculatus*) another small wildflower has yellow petals tinged with red, hence known as 'bacon-and-eggs'.

Sheep's sorrel (*Rumex acetosella*) distinguished by its red 'haze' when in flower in May (large patches may be seen north of Holly (Bog) Lodge.

Mouse-ear hawkweed (*Pilosella officinarum)*, usually only 10 - 15 centimetres high, with yellow flowers, common in short turf and on anthills.

Harebells (*Campanula rotundifolia*), a late summer grassland delight.

Native bluebells (*Hyacynthoides nonscriptus*).

Heath bedstraw (*Galium saxatile*), for which anthills are a favourite location.

Common (but actually uncommon) **or heath speedwell** (*Veronica officinalis*).

4. NUTRIENT ENRICHED AREAS

Principal locations: Petersham Park and slopes and areas of recent disturbance or localised nutrient enrichment (e.g. canine faeces/urine). These areas are characterised by coarse grasses. The most significant fact, perhaps, is that at least two of the coarse grasses which dominate these areas, **Timothy grass** or **common cat's tail** (*Phleum pratense*) and **cocksfoot** (*Dactylis glomerata*), were not here when Charles I enclosed the park. They were both imported from America in the mid-eighteenth century for agricultural purposes. Natives include **Yorkshire fog** (*Holcus lanatus*); and **red fescue**. As for the grass on the playing fields, this is common **rye grass** (*Lolium perenne*), the stuff we use for our lawns. It is probably an exotic, first on record as sown in Britain in 1677. Bearing in mind that there were some forty football pitches in the park in the 1920s, there must be a lot of rye grass elsewhere.

5. SCARCER PLANTS

Native black poplars (*Populus nigra* ssp. *betulifolia*): good examples are (i) in the gully by the park wall between Cambrian Road and Bog Gates (Tree No.1075) and (ii) about 100m east of Sheen Cottage, against the wall (Tree No.1094); just north of Ham Cross Plantation there is a sizeable community of **upright chickweed**, scarce nationally. At the south end of the upper pen pond **ivy-leafed winter crowfoot** grows, very rare for Greater London. **Lesser skull-cap** occurs beside several ponds and this, too, is rare. On the old boundary bank of Rutnells there still grows a veteran **crab apple** (*Malus silvestris,* Tree No.1396), the only one publicly accessible. Crab apples are singletons, found occasionally in woodland and very old hedgerows, as in this case.

APPENDIX 2

The deer and the birds

This section deals only with the deer, introduced with the enclosure, and with birds.

THE DEER

There are about 350 fallow and 300 red deer in the park. They normally feed off grass, rushes, sedges, acorns, chestnuts, beech mast (or nuts), fungi, tree foliage, bark and grass and hay. The open landscape of the park is thus thanks to the voracious habit of the deer, clearing virtually all the cover from the ground and also creating a 'browse line' defining the base level of foliage on trees. During the winter months the deer receive a supplementary feed each night, feed being dispersed to each herd from the back of a moving vehicle, thereby ensuring that all deer have access.

Fallow males are called bucks and females does, but red deer males are called stags (or harts) and females hinds. Newborn fallow deer are fawns, but new born red deer are calves.

For about ten months of the year mature males of both species remain apart from mature females, calves/fawns and yearlings. Young males stay with the female herd until they are about 20 months old when they become mature and join the bucks or stags, but the mature females evict yearling stags for the duration of the rut, sometimes literally kicking them out.

Fallow deer This is the most widely distributed of six species of deer in Britain. There is evidence of fallow deer in Britain before the last Ice Age, 150,000 years ago, but they became extinct. They were reintroduced in the historic period, and some thirty herds were recorded in the Domesday Book.

The park's fallow deer are of two types, menil and common. Both are coloured rich fawn with white spots in summer, but in winter the menil do not lose their spots entirely while the common fallow go dark fawn or grey and their spots virtually disappear. They may be distinguished in winter, the menil having a brown patch on their hindquarters and the common having a black patch on theirs.

Red deer The stags usually gather in groups of less than 20, with a dominance hierarchy based on age/strength. This hierarchy is usually established by gestures rather than overt threat. Higher ranking stags are likely to be 7-12 years old, carrying 13 or 15 point antlers or more (see below). In late September these groups break up as the stags go off singly in search of hinds. Red deer can live for up to 25 years, though by 1996 one hind had unusually reached the age of 27.

Rutting The rutting season for both red and fallow deer peaks in the last fortnight of October. Mating normally takes place at night but the pattern for fallow and red deer ruts is significantly different.

(i) Red stags round up as many hinds as possible in their 'hareem', migrate to a rutting area, and fight off challengers, a process of natural selection whereby hinds are impregnated by the strongest stags. The 'fights' are dramatic as stags lock antlers and seek to defeat their competitor in what are essentially trials of strength. By the end of the rutting season a red stag's antlers tips will be whitened from wear and tear in combat, and sometimes antler tips will be broken.

(ii) By contrast, fallow bucks wait for the does to come to them. They mark their rutting stands (roughly half an acre in size), scraping in the ground, and anointing the ground and trees with urine or rutty odour from their musk glands (below the eye) to attract does. They seldom keep a hareem. It is easy to locate the stands during or after rutting, for the areas are heavily scraped.

For example there are two stands just below the escarpment, one above Sudbrook Park, and another between Ham and Kingston Gates. Some of the rutting stands in the park are over a century old, successive bucks fighting to inherit the stand from their predecessors.

Fawning For both species gestation is 8 months, and within 20 minutes of birth a calf/fawn can walk, and in two days can run at the heels of its mother. Particularly soon after fawning, does (but not hinds) will signal danger by barking and 'pronking': bouncing stiff legged before running away. Hinds often return to the site of their own birth when calving. They can be aggressively protective during calving, and dogs that approach too closely may be attacked. Ham Cross Wood is particularly to be avoided in June.

The cull Males are culled in February, and females in November, just after the rut. Up to a maximum of 200 deer are culled each year, depending on the birth rate and casualties, in order to keep the population stable, healthy, and with a good age structure, and the venison sold for market.

Antlers In early spring, about 8 months after birth, lumps form on the pedicles, the permanent bony structures on the front of the skull from which the antlers grow. These are covered in 'velvet', the membrane that carries blood and oxygen for antler growth, which is shed in late summer when the antler is mature. The antlers themselves are shed annually in March. New antlers are soft, even slightly flexible. At 15 months a fallow male (technically known as a 'pricket') has unbranched spikes but thereafter grows 'palmate antlers. With the red deer, the number of antler points (or 'tines') broadly indicates age. The largest pair of antlers can exceed 12 points and can weigh 9kg, no less than half the weight of the skeleton. Very occasionally a 28 point deer will be seen in the park, an indication of the almost pampered life enjoyed in the park. The park record is a 29 point stag (sadly struck by a car and put down). In old age the antlers diminish each year in size and points, rather like veteran oaks.

Deer pens The primary purpose of deer pens was to provide supplementary feeding for deer, necessary with the larger herds in previous centuries. Two pens survive, a nineteenth century wooden enclosure north of the White Lodge and an open greensward on the edge of the deer sanctuary in High Wood, both worth looking at if you are passing by. Deer pens were surrounded by post and rail fencing with gaps wide enough for deer to enter but too narrow for cattle. Inside the deer pen would be a smaller enclosure that allowed in only the fawns.

Fenced paddocks or pens would also be used by the keepers to catch deer, dogs being used to drive a selected animal into an opening which would be netted on the far side, where the deer would become entangled. An alternative method was to bring a deer to bay using hounds trained to seize it by the throat and ears and hold it down for the keepers to tie its legs. Now they are shot.

A SHORT HISTORY OF DEER IN RICHMOND PARK

Deer were first kept and fed in the 'Great Paddock' (now the golf course) on the east side of Beverley Brook. By the time of the 1660 Restoration there were some 2,000 deer, but within nine years Charles II was complaining that only 600 were left, partly the result of his hunting but more the result of thefts by park staff particularly of the fawns.

During the eighteenth century there was a shift from hunting and killing to hunting and releasing deer. However, stags used for several hunts became aggressive, and deer hunting fell into abeyance in the second half of the century in favour of venison farming.

In 1831 Edward Jesse made a detailed survey of the deer, the first since 1669, by which time while there were 1,400 fallow deer there were only 50 red deer left. Intensive management and enlargement of the fallow and red herds took place, so that by 1850 there were 1,500 deer again. However, in 1871, a review of the cost of providing venison for the royal household established a cost per carcase in Richmond Park at £9.14s, an uneconomic cost. Rather than remove the herds, however,

> 'The Lords Commissioners considering the great addition which the presence of the herds make to the beauty of the Parks are not prepared to direct that they should be removed.'

In 1886 unusual behaviour among the fallow deer near East Sheen Gate was diagnosed as rabies, the first authenticated case in Britain. By September of the following year 264 fallow deer had been lost, but the epidemic was contained thanks largely to the fact that fallow herds are relatively static, and other herds in the park escaped the infection virtually unscathed.

The next peril for the deer was world war, when the demand for meat left the park with approximately 400 fallow and 50 red deer. With so many troops using the park it is a moot point how often beef stew tasted extraordinarily like venison.

Currently the fallow and red herds are about 350 and 300 strong respectively. Reduction of the car speed limit has reduced the annual deer death by motorists from about 20-30 deer to only three or four. Another 20 deer, or so, are attacked annually by dogs.

BIRDS

Sixty years ago 133 different species of bird were listed as residents or visitors to the park. There has been a 9 per cent loss since then, with something in the order of 120 species still to be seen. However, of these barely 50 are permanent residents, and the remainder are seasonal migrants and a handful of rare strays.

There is the changing balance of species. For example, the currently ubiquitous magpie could be described in 1937 as 'an occasional visitor to the park occurrences usually take place during the winter months.' A century earlier on the other hand Edward Jesse wrote of 'constant fights between the Mistletoe Thrush and the Magpie.' Likewise there were only a few crows in 1900. A flock of 20 were worthy of mention in 1927 but a decade later one of 40 was not unusual. Unfortunately they have never looked back. They are a growing problem, living off human litter, bread fed to waterfowl and canine faeces. They inhibit the proliferation of other species, raiding the nests of smaller birds. Thrushes of all kinds are now rarer than they were only a few years ago, and both house and tree sparrows once so common are now hardly seen at all. Skylarks, yellow hammers and redstarts have all declined partly as a result of the heavy dog presence. Because dogs must be leashed in it, the Isabella Plantation is perhaps the best place to look out for birds. (refer to the bird listing in Walk No.11).

BIRDS TO LOOK OUT FOR IN THE PARK

There are a basic number of easily recognizable birds which will delight the eye.

Green Woodpeckers (or Yaffles) are very common, particularly since they make an easy living from the anthills in the park.

Great and Lesser Spotted Woodpeckers are rarer, but can be seen in the Isabella Plantation, Sidmouth and Conduit woods. The Great Spotted is easily detectable for the rapid hammer drill sound of its beak. The Lesser Spotted, a nineteenth century introduction, was decimated by the winters of 1947/48 and 1962/63. Its population has still not fully recovered.

Kingfishers may be seen on Beverley Brook, and on the Pen Ponds, and in the autumn in the Isabella Plantation, though they are shy and so swift in flight one may see nothing but a streak of electric blue.

Ring-necked parakeets, escaped from captivity, may be spotted in the park, particularly along Beverley Brook. They are yellow-green and long tailed, with an orange-red half collar each side of the neck and a crimson beak.

Herons fish in most of the park's ponds. The heronry is in Pond Plantation on the south side of the Upper Pen Pond and may be observed from the north side of the Pond.

Kestrels are easily identified as the only British birds of prey which hover over open ground. Their population fluctuates considerably.

Sparrowhawks are plentiful but harder to spot, since ambush is their stock-in-trade. They usually hunt in woodland clearings. With short powerful rounded wings, they can match the speed, twists and turns of their prey. Far easier to see than the bird itself are the remains of their prey, for they pluck their kill. Scattered feathers are a frequent sight on the ground, evidence that the sparrowhawk is alive and well in the park.

Tawny and Little Owls are both found in the park. These are most easily spotted at dusk, when they begin hunting. Tawny Owls favour ancient pollards for nesting.

Skylarks: their numbers plummeted by 55 per cent between 1974 and 1999, have now stabilised but not regained their former number.

Waders – for example, *sandpipers, ringed plovers, redshanks, greenshanks* and sometimes even *curlews* – can been seen on the Pen Ponds in spring and autumn, the best seasons for keeping an eye open for migrating birds.

From April to August *swifts, swallows, house and sand martins* may be seen in the park. Their superlative flying may be enjoyed at the Pen Ponds where there are plenty of airborne insects for them to feed off.

Ducks, on the pond in Isabella Plantation, but often elsewhere: *Coots, Mallards, Moorhens, Shovelers, Gadwalls, Common Pochards, Red-crested Pochards, Northern Pintails, Tufted Ducks, European Wigeons*, and two naturalised exotics: *Egyptian Geese* and *Mandarins*. Furthermore, there are those uninvited guests, now become indigenous, the Canada geese.

APPENDIX 3

The ponds

A number of natural water courses predate the enclosure:

(i) The main one is **Beverley Brook** (which rises in Worcester Park) and its three feeders running down from Pond Slade, Sidmouth Wood and from the valley between Barn Wood and Sawpit Plantation.

(ii) **Sudbrook** which drains the spring above Dann's Pond not far from Ladderstile Gate, down through the gully to Ham Dip, and thence through Ham Gate Pond to Sudbrook Park.

(iii) **A stream**, known in the nineteenth century as 'The Black Ditch', running north from Sidmouth Wood, through Conduit Wood to the park wall, being the parish boundary between Richmond and Mortlake.

In addition there were a number of springs, of which the most notable is the White Conduit in Conduit Wood, tapped in about 1500 for the Royal Palace. There were also a number of small ponds and one large one by Roehampton Gate, still in existence in the mid-eighteenth century. Other ponds, for example in front of the Old Lodge, and by Bog and Richmond Gates, came and went, as can be seen on John Eyre's map of 1754 , p.86-87.

Most of today's ponds are either inundated gravel pits, or were specially dug to assist draining and provide water for the livestock. We do not know the precise dates when many of these were dug, but the following dates indicate the first mapped record:

Adam's 1754
BarnWood........................ 1861
Bishop's........................... 1861
Conduit Wood.................. 1861

Dann's	1754
Gallows	1861
Ham Dip (or Glen)	1861
Ham Gate	1754
Leg of Mutton	1637
Martin's	1861
Peg's	1861
Pens	1746
Spanker's Hill	1850
Still	1861
Thomson's	1955
White Ash	1861

Leg of Mutton is the original pen pond (still known as such in 1876), and eighteenth century maps show the presently named Pen Ponds as 'The Canal'. All those ponds dug in 1861 represent part of the first effective attempt to deal with the widespread boggy areas in the park by Josiah Parkes, and to provide more adequate deer drinking facilities (Walk No.7).

Index